ILLUSTRATED JUNIOR

MATHEMATICS

Dictionary

BY
BRYN ROBERTS

Illustrated junior mathematics dictionary

263194
Non-Fiction   510 ROB
Royal Grammar School Guildford

Published by Pearson Education Limited, Edinburgh Gate, Harlow, Essex, CM20 2JE.

www.pearsonschoolsandfecolleges.co.uk

Text © Pearson Education Limited 2011
Edited by Jenny Oates
Proofread by Janice Curry
Designed and typeset by Scout Design
Original illustrations © Pearson Education Ltd 2011
Illustrated by Tech Type
Cover design by Scout Design
Picture research by Kevin Brown

First published 2011

15 14 13 12 11
IMP 10 9 8 7 6 5 4 3 2 1

British Library Cataloguing in Publication Data
A catalogue record for this book is available from the British Library

ISBN 978 0 435 07457 9

Copyright notice
All rights reserved. No part of this publication may be reproduced in any form or by any means (including photocopying or storing it in any medium by electronic means and whether or not transiently or incidentally to some other use of this publication) without the written permission of the copyright owner, except in accordance with the provisions of the Copyright, Designs and Patents Act 1988 or under the terms of a licence issued by the Copyright Licensing Agency, Saffron House, 6¬–10 Kirby Street, London EC1N 8TS (www.cla.co.uk). Applications for the copyright owner's written permission should be addressed to the publisher.

Printed in Spain by Graficas Estella

Acknowledgements
The publisher would like to thank the following for their kind permission to reproduce their photographs:

(Key: b-bottom; c-centre; l-left; r-right; t-top)

Alamy Images: Carole Hewer 30, GONDWANA PHOTO ART 38, Ian Francis 40l, ICP 40c, imagebroker 35, INTERFOTO 64, Mary Evans Picture Library 93, PjrStudio 23l, Stock Connection Blue 59t, Ted Foxx 33; **Corbis**: Philip Wallick / AgStock Images 6, Stefano Bianchetti 3t; **Fotolia.com**: Andrei Nekrassov 2l, Andy Rhodes 56b, Angel Simon 82cr, Artur Synenko 10, Asbe 79, caimacanul 17, Carina Hansen 21, Coprid 58b, dinostock 72r, Elena Moiseeva 67, Elenathewise 36, evgenyi 65, fat*fa*tin 29, gemphotography 25, Graphic design 71t, Horticulture 24, 66t, itestro 57, jamalludin din 82tl, Jaren Wicklund 3b, Jon Le-Bon 86r, Justimagine 71b, KtD 82b, Mark J. Grenier 86l, mark yuill 60, Maxim Loskutnikov 56t, milosluz 7r, Oleg Seleznev 59b, papajka 82cl, Patrik Winbjörk 87t, Paul Maguire 91, Paul Moore 58t, Richard Blaker 34b, Rohit Seth 73, 80l, 80r, Scanrail 70, Surflifes 23r, Tom Hirtreiter 82tr, Yuri Arcurs 7l; **Getty Images**: Antenna Audio, Inc. 72l; **Glow Images**: Imagesource 9; **iStockphoto**: Ekaterina Monakhova 2r, jsemeniuk 44; **Pearson Education Ltd**: Brand X Pictures. Joe Atlas 4, 52, 66c, Gareth Dewar 40r, 62, Photodisc. Photolink 47; **Shutterstock.com**: BsWei 5, Offscreen 66b, Scott Leman 87b, slpix 34t

Cover images: Front: **Alamy Images**: ICP; Corbis: Stefano Bianchetti; **Fotolia.com**: Jon Le-Bon, Surflifes, Tom Hirtreiter; Back: **Fotolia.com**: Artur Synenko, Graphic design; **Shutterstock.com**: slpix

All other images © Pearson Education

Every effort has been made to trace the copyright holders and we apologise in advance for any unintentional omissions. We would be pleased to insert the appropriate acknowledgement in any subsequent edition of this publication.

Introduction

Welcome to the new **Illustrated Junior Maths Dictionary** from Pearson Education. We hope that you find it useful. The terms we have included are those you might need to use as you study mathematics in primary or junior school.

Each entry has a similar structure as shown below:

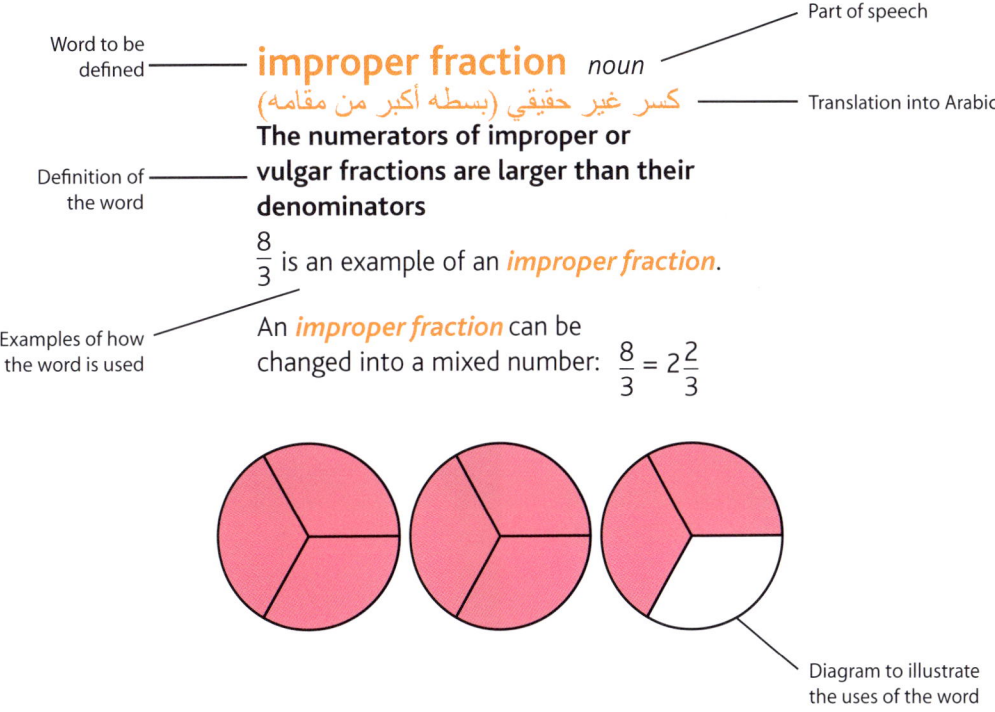

Word to be defined

Part of speech

improper fraction *noun*

كسر غير حقيقي (بسطه أكبر من مقامه) — Translation into Arabic

Definition of the word

The numerators of improper or vulgar fractions are larger than their denominators

$\frac{8}{3}$ is an example of an *improper fraction*.

Examples of how the word is used

An *improper fraction* can be changed into a mixed number: $\frac{8}{3} = 2\frac{2}{3}$

Diagram to illustrate the uses of the word

This dictionary is also available as a digital product on CD-ROM, if you prefer to use a newer way of checking the meanings of these words. The digital version also includes audio tracks (in British and American English) of all the words and definitions, some word games and activities and simulations of some of the words in the dictionary. It is quick and fun to use. To order the digital version contact your usual bookseller quoting the ISBN on the back cover of this book.

i

Aa

abacus noun   مِعدَاد

Apparatus used by early civilisations and in more recent times, before electronic instruments were invented, for calculations; now used as an educational aid in representing numbers

Some shopkeepers in some parts of Asia still use an *abacus* to do their accounting.

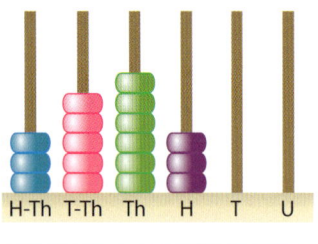

This 6-spike school *abacus* shows the approximate distance from the Earth to the Moon. That is, 356 300 km.

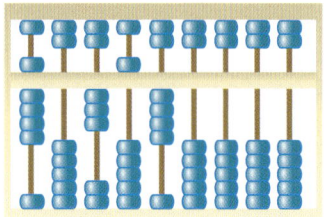

This Chinese *abacus* uses a more complex system. It shows 903 540 000. Such abacuses were used for adding and subtracting before electronic calculators were invented.

addition noun

The process of calculating the total of two or more numbers

In 14 + 23 + 36 = 73, 14, 23 and 36 are addends and 73 is the total.
'+' is the *addition* sign, also referred to as the 'plus sign' and '=' is the equals sign. For their homework, the teacher set the students 20 *addition* exercises, so that they could practise adding numbers together.
See signs

algebra noun

A branch of mathematics that uses symbols and letters to represent numbers and quantities

Algebra can be used to find the values of U and x in:

$6 + U = 9$ $8 + x = 12$
$7 - U = 4$ $15 - x = 10$

analogue

algorithm
noun خوارزمية / طريقة حساب

Step-by-step routine procedure by which an operation, such as addition, subtraction, multiplication or division can be systematically carried out to a conclusion

The Rubik's cube puzzle toy can be solved using a series of *algorithms*.

See addition, division, multiplication, subtraction

altitude *noun* ارتفاع

A line through one vertex and perpendicular to the opposite side of a triangle

The three *altitudes* of a triangle meet at the orthocentre.
The lines BD and CE are *altitudes.*

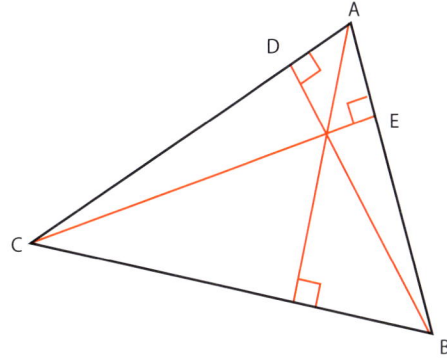

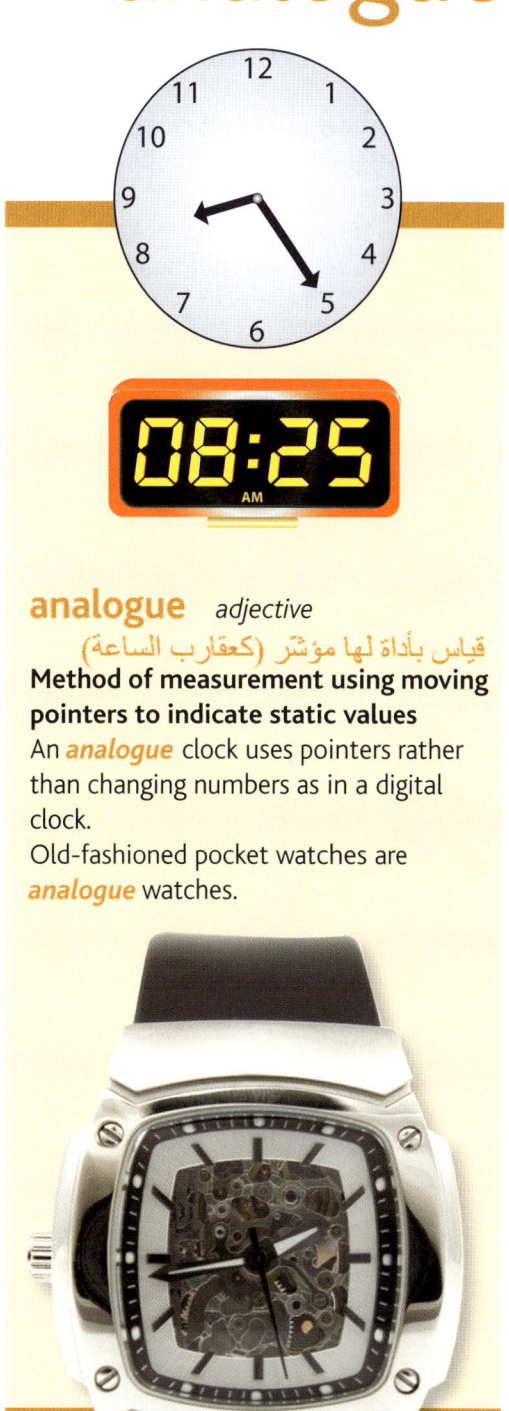

analogue *adjective*
قياس بأداة لها مؤشّر (كعقارب الساعة)

Method of measurement using moving pointers to indicate static values

An *analogue* clock uses pointers rather than changing numbers as in a digital clock.
Old-fashioned pocket watches are *analogue* watches.

3

angle

angle *noun* زاوية

The amount of turn of a line segment from its original position about a fixed point

Angles are measured in degrees (°).
A complete turn is 360° or four right *angles*.
A right *angle* is 90°.

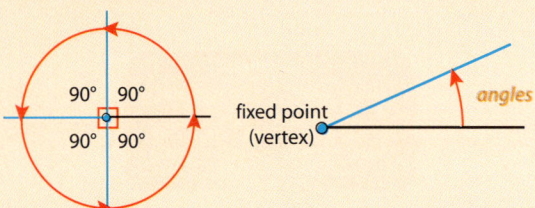

Angles are named using three letters.
∠ AOB and ∠ BOC lie next to each other.
∠ AOB and ∠ BOC are adjacent *angles*.
The corners of a room meet at an *angle*.
The back of a chair is set at an *angle* to the seat.

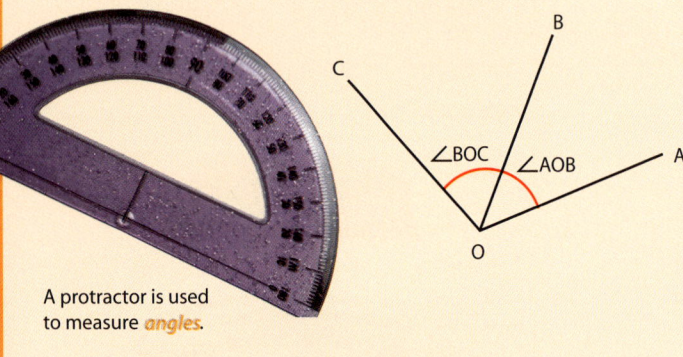

A protractor is used to measure *angles*.

angle types   أنواع الزوايا

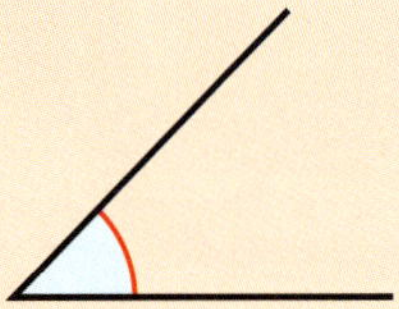

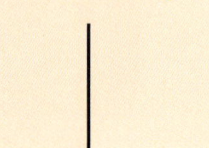

Acute *angle*: less than 90°.

Right *angle*: 90°.

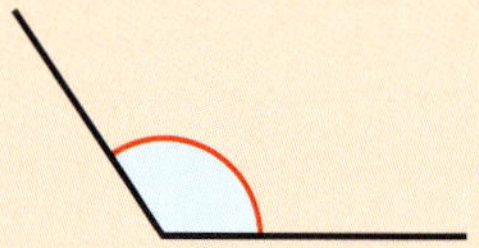

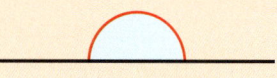

Obtuse *angle*: between 90° and 180°.

Straight *angle*: 180°.

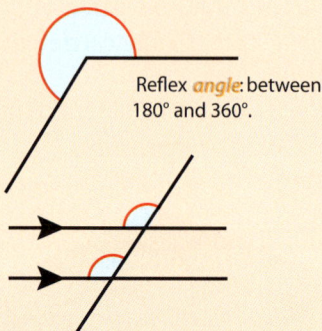

Reflex *angle*: between 180° and 360°.

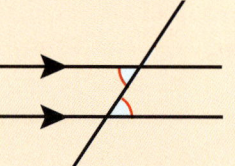

Corresponding *angles* are equal.

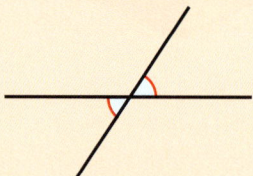

Alternate *angles* are equal.

Vertically opposite *angles* are equal.

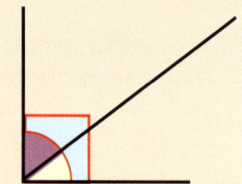

Complementary *angles* add up to 90°.

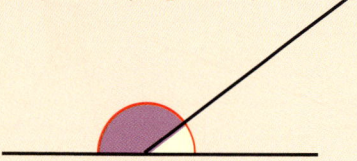

Supplementary *angles* add up to 180°.

See constructions

anticlockwise   adjective   عكس عقارب الساعة

The opposite to clockwise, i.e. moving in the opposite direction to the direction that a clock's hands move

If you are asked to walk around the classroom in an *anticlockwise* direction, you will find that you are always turning to the left.
See clockwise

applied   adjective   تطبيقي

Applied mathematics is a branch of mathematics which deals with practical matters such as bridge construction and space technology

In contrast to *applied* mathematics, pure mathematics is a study of systems and structures in the abstract.
See pure mathematics

approximation   noun   تقريب

Approximation can be stated in various ways:
- rounded to the nearest whole number;
- rounded to the nearest 10, 100, 1000 etc.;
- correct to 1, 2, 3 etc. decimal places;
- correct to 1, 2, 3 etc. significant figures

The sign for *approximation* is ≈
See decimal, round

$$97 \approx 100 \qquad 4.36 \approx 4.4$$

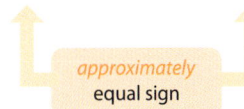
approximately equal sign

area

arc   noun   قوس

Part of a circle or curve, a non-straight line

A rounded arch under a bridge has edges which are curves, like an *arc*. The red lines below are all *arcs*.

are   noun

الآر: وحدة مساحة مقدارها مائة متر مربع

A metric measurement of area
The area of a field can be measured in *ares*.
See hectare

area   noun   مساحة

The amount of surface

The *areas* of countries are given in square kilometres (km²).
The *area* of farm land is usually written in hectares (ha).
There are various formulae for calculating the *area* of different shapes.
See formulae

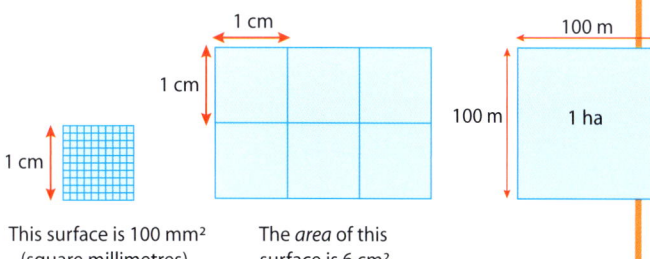

This surface is 100 mm² (square millimetres). 100 mm² = 1 cm²

The *area* of this surface is 6 cm² (square centimetres).

arithmetic

arithmetic noun   علم الحساب
The branch of mathematics which deals with numbers, the processing of numbers and measurement; it also includes solving word problems and money
For example, if you went to the shop to buy some sweets, you would need to work out how many you could buy with the money that you have. You would use *arithmetic* to do this.

arithmetic mean noun   الوسط الحسابي
The arithmetic mean, mean or average, of a set of values is the sum or total of the values divided by the number of values
For example; the test scores of a pupil in four tests were: 5, 6, 6, 7.

$$\text{mean} = \frac{\text{sum of scores}}{\text{number of scores}}$$

$$= \frac{5+6+6+7}{4} = \frac{24}{4} = 6$$

The *arithmetic mean* of 5, 6, 6 and 7 is 6.

arithmetic progression (AP) noun   متوالية عددية
A sequence of numbers or terms, each differing by a common difference from the previous number; for example 4, 8, 12, 16, 20
In this *arithmetic progression* the common difference between each term and the next is 4. So the 6th term will be 24. Calculating the 6th term:
First term + (6 - 1) terms x common difference
$$4 + 5 \times 4 = 24$$

7th term $= 4 + (7 - 1)4$
$= 4 + 6 \times 4 = 4 + 24 = 28$

array noun   مصفوفة
An arrangement of objects or numbers in rows and columns
You can see many examples in the world around you, for instance the seats in a cinema are often set out in rows and columns, making an *array*.
When tins are stacked neatly on the shelves in a supermarket, they form an *array*.

ascending adjective   تصاعدي
Literally means 'going up' and in mathematics refers to the order within a group of values; so anything that is arranged from smallest to largest, or lowest to highest, is arranged in ascending order
For example, this set of numbers: 78, 53, 12, 92, 27, 97, 45 can be arranged in *ascending* order – from smallest to largest: 12, 27, 45, 53, 78, 92, 97.
If the children in a class were asked to line up in order of age, with the youngest at the front and the oldest at the back, they would line up in *ascending* order of age.
See descending

associative law

noun   الخاصية التجميعية

The associative laws for addition and multiplication state that when three or more numbers are added or multiplied the sum or product is the same regardless of the order of the numbers

For example whichever order 2 + 5 + 8 are added in the result is always 15.

(2 + 5) + 8	2 + (5 × 8)
= 7 + 8	= 2 × 40
= 15	= 80

Whichever order 2 × 5 × 8 are multiplied in the answer is always 80.

(2 × 5) × 8	2 × (5 × 8)
= 10 × 8	= 2 × 40
= 80	= 80

See commutative, distributive laws

asymmetry

noun   عدم التماثل

The opposite of symmetry

The letter 'O' can be folded so that each side is the same. The fold is a line of symmetry. Letter 'Q' cannot be folded so that each side is the same. Letter Q is *asymmetrical*.
See symmetry

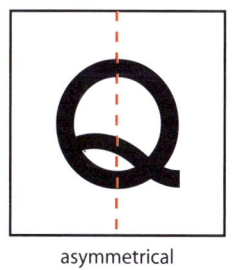
asymmetrical

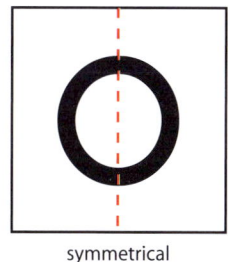
symmetrical

axis

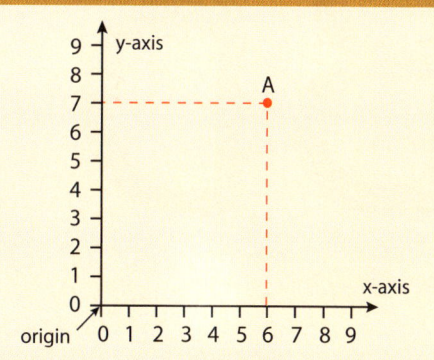

axis   noun   محور

Either of the two straight lines of a graph

The horizontal *x-axis* and the vertical *y-axis* are a graph's *axes* of reference. For example, by referring to the scales on the *x* and *y axis*, the postion of A can be given as (6,7). The *x-axis* reference, known as the *x* coordinate, is always written first.

axis (rotation)

noun   محور (دوران)

A line about which an object rotates

For example, the Earth spins on its *axis*.
A gyroscope is designed to spin on its axis in order to balance.

axis (symmetry)

noun   محور (تماثل)

A straight line about which any symmetrical shape can be folded

The *axis* in a symmetrical shape is also called a line of symmetry.

7

Bb

bar chart noun   رسم بياني بالأعمدة / مخطط أعمدة

A bar chart or bar graph has vertical or horizontal bars, with spaces between the columns; the information or data shown by the bars are usually the result of data gathering or a survey

The *bar chart* below shows the cost of generating 1 kWh of power in different types of power stations.
See graphs

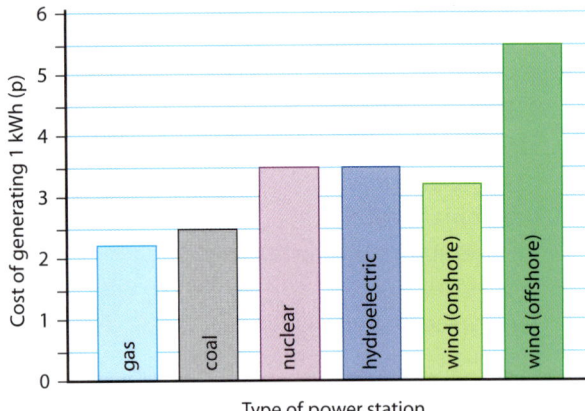

base noun   قاعدة

The grouping number for a counting system

All counting systems have a number *base*. We normally use *base* 10 for counting. It has 10 digits – 0, 1, 2, 3, 4, 5, 6, 7, 8 and 9 which are used to make up all numbers in the system.

Computer technology uses *base* 2 or the binary system. It has 2 digits – 0 and 1. Values in one number *base* can be converted to another:

```
    100                    128 64 32 16 8 4 2 1
    10
    1
   1 3 5          = 1 0 0 0 0 1 1 1
1 × 100 = 100  Base 10    1 × 128 = 128   Base 2
3 × 10  =  30             0 × 64  =   0
5 × 1   =   5 +           0 × 32  =   0
          ───             0 × 16  =   0
          135             0 × 8   =   0
                          1 × 4   =   4
                          1 × 2   =   2
                          1 × 1   =   1
                                    ───
                                    135
```

bell-curve noun   منحنى جرسي

The line produced on a frequency diagram illustrating normal distribution
See normal distribution

```
                    Thousand-millions
                     Hundred-millions
                       Ten-millions
                         Millions
                      Hundred-thousands
                       Ten-thousands
                         Thousands
                         Hundreds
                           Tens
                          Units
1 Billion ⟶  1 0 0 0 0 0 0 0 0 0
```

billion noun   بليون / مليار

A billion is a number with a place value of one thousand million at one time a thousand million was called a milliard
1 000 000 000 can also be written as 10^9. The Earth is about 5 billion years old.
See decimal

brackets

binomial adjective   ذو حدَّين
An expression which has two terms, such as 3*a* + 2*b* or 2*x* - 3*y*

bi- as a prefix means 'two'. For example, bilateral means having two sides, someone who speaks English and Arabic equally well is bilingual; a bicycle is so-called because it has two wheels.

bisect verb   ينصّف
To cut into to two equal parts; if you cut an orange exactly in two, you have bisected it

The angle shown here is a *bisected* angle as it has been cut into two equal parts.

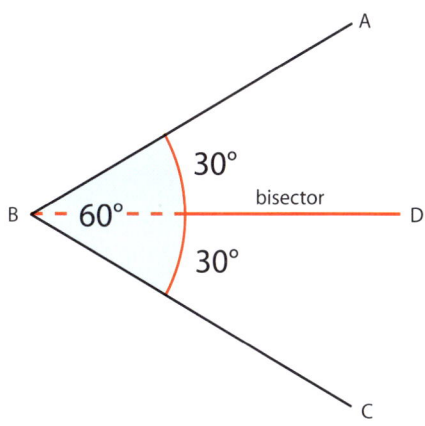

$\angle$ ABC = 60°
BD is the *bisector* of $\angle$ ABC.
$\angle$ ABD = $\angle$ CBD
$\angle$ ABD = 30° and $\angle$ CBD = 30°.

BODMAS
abbreviation   ترتيب العمليات الحسابية
See *order of operations*

boundary noun
The line around the perimeter of flat or two-dimensional (2D) shapes

The *boundary* of the school grounds is often marked by a wall or a fence.
See *perimeter*

brackets noun   أقواس
Brackets ( ) and square brackets [ ] are pairs of symbols for grouping terms within an expression

For example:

2 + (8 x 3)	(2 + 8) x 3	[(2 + 8) x 3]²
= 2 + 24	= 10 x 3	= [10 x 3]²
= 26	= 30	= 900

Curly brackets
{ } can be used to denote a set, for example:
P = {odd numbers}
Q = {2, 4, 6, 8, 10}
R = {3, 6, 9, 12, ... }
See *order of operations*, *symbols*

9

Cc

calculate   verb   يحسب

The procedure for getting the answer.
The answer in:
- addition is called a sum or total;
- subtraction is called the difference;
- multiplication is called the product;
- division is called the quotient

When your teacher gives you a set of sums to do, she is asking you to *calculate* the answers.

calculator   noun   آلة حاسبة

An electronic device used to work out a mathematical problem
Scientific *calculators* use the perfect algebraic method. This means that expressions such as:
$(2 + 7)^2 + (5 - 3)^3$
can be entered using the appropriate keys. Students are sometimes allowed to use *calculators* in their exams. Accountants use *calculators* to help them with their work.

calendar   noun   تقويم

Arrangement of days, weeks and months for a particular year
This poem helps us remember how the $365\frac{1}{4}$ days of a non-leap year are ordered into named months:

Thirty days has September,
April, June and November.
All the rest have thirty-one
Except February alone,
Which has twenty-eight days clear
And twenty-nine in each leap year.

A leap year occurs every 4 years and its number is divisible by 4. So far, in this century the leap years are 2000, 2004, 2008, 2012 …
Calendars come in many shapes and sizes, but they all show the month, date and day, so that people can use them to organise their lives.
Nowadays many people use electronic *calendars* on their computers or even on their mobile phones.

cancelling   noun   حذف

The procedure for reducing a fraction to its lowest terms. The numerator and denominator of a fraction are divided by their greatest common factor

Numerator	$\frac{18 \div 9}{27 \div 9} = \frac{2}{3}$	$\frac{18^2}{27^3} = \frac{2}{3}$
Denominator		

Before *cancelling* (verb) a fraction, you will have to find the greatest common factor of the numerator and the denominator.
See reduce

10

centi-

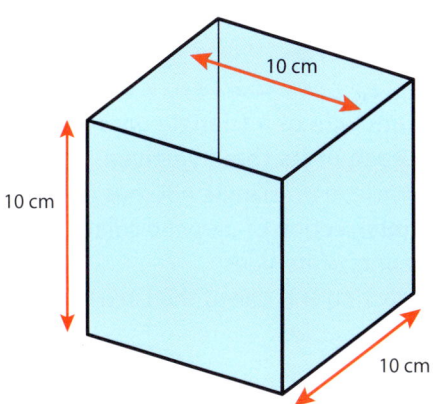

The *capacity* of this cube is 1000 cubic centimetres (cm³) or 1 litre.

capacity noun   سعة

The amount a container will hold; capacity is measured in litres (l) and millilitres (ml)

A cubic container with internal measurements of 10 cm has a *capacity* of 1l of liquid.

If you pour 2 litres of any liquid into a 2-litre measuring jug, it will be filled to *capacity*.

If the seating *capacity* of a bus is stated as 75 people, that means that seating for 75 people only is available.

cardinal number
noun   عدد أصلي

Any number expressing quantity, so 1, 2, 3, 4 ... are all cardinal numbers

The *cardinal* number of set A is 3 because it has 3 members.

Set A

carrying (addition)
noun   الحمل (عملية الجمع)

Name given to the process, in addition, of 'renaming and transferring' any column total, greater than 9, to the next column

$$\begin{array}{r} 2\,3\,7 \\ +\,{}_14\,{}_19\,8 \\ \hline 7\,3\,5 \end{array}$$

What we say:
7 + 8 = 15. Write 5, *carry* 1.
1 + 3 + 9 = 13. Write 3,
1 + 2 + 4 = 7. Write 7.

What we mean:
7 + 8 = 15 ones
15 ones = 1 ten + 5 ones
Write 5, *carry* 1 Ten.

1 + 3 + 9 = 13 tens. 13 tens = 1 hundred + 3 tens. Write 3, *carry* 1 hundred.

1 + 2 + 4 = 7 hundreds. Write 7.

In addition, when the sum for a column is greater than 9, *carrying* is used to transfer the appropriate multiple to the next column on the left.

centi-
prefix   سنتي: بادئة بمعنى جزء من مئة

Metric system prefix for $\frac{1}{100}$.
100 *centi*metre = 1 metre   100 cm = 1 m
1 cm = $\frac{1}{100}$ m, 1 cm = 0.01 m

*Centi*pedes are so-called because they were thought to have 100 legs.

centroid

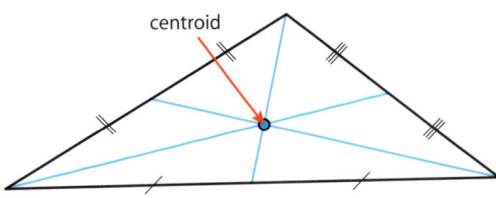

centroid
noun نقطة تقاطع متوسطات المثلث

A roughly central point in a triangle which makes the intersection of the triangle's medians

The medians of a triangle meet at its *centroid*.
A median is a straight line from a vertex to the midpoint of the opposite side.
See median

chord *noun* وتر

A straight line from arc to arc of a circle that does not pass through the centre of the circle; it divides the circle into a major and minor segment

Below is a diagram showing a *chord*.

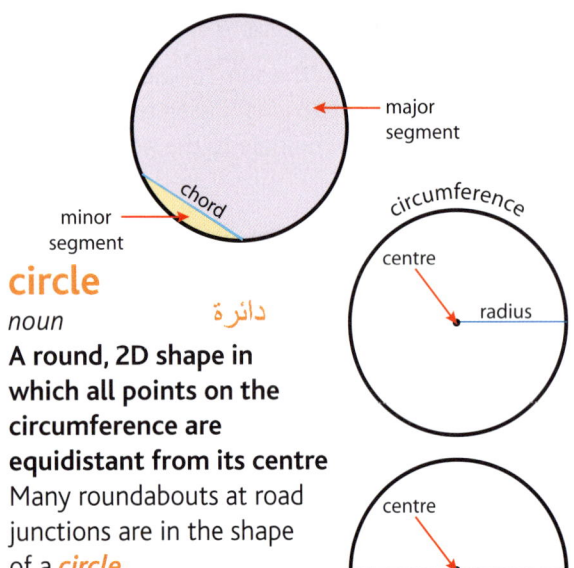

circle
noun دائرة

A round, 2D shape in which all points on the circumference are equidistant from its centre

Many roundabouts at road junctions are in the shape of a *circle*.
See plane or 2D shapes

circumcircle
noun دائرة مارة برؤوس مضلع

The circumcircle of a triangle passes through each of its three vertices

The circumcircle of triangle ABC has its centre D at the intersection of perpendiculars from the midpoints of its sides.
The intersection D is called the circumcentre of the *circumcircle*.

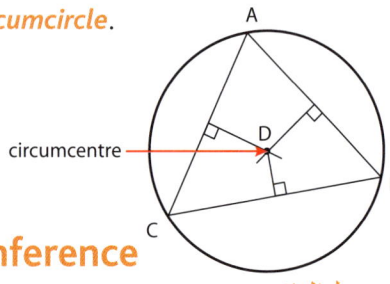

circumference
noun محيط الدائرة

The perimeter or outer edge of a circle is termed its circumference

For example, if a plate has a *circumference* of 50 cm, that would mean that it measures 50 cm all the way around.
If you want to know how big your waist is, you need to measure its *circumference*.
See circle

clockwise
adjective في اتجاه عقارب الساعة

Movement in the same direction as the hands of an analogue clock

If you walk around something in a *clockwise* direction you will find that you are always turning to the right.
See anticlockwise

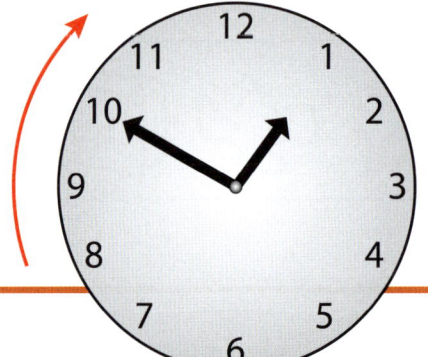

common ratio

collinear
adjective   على استقامة واحدة

Points which lie on the same straight line are collinear; in this diagram, points A, B and C are collinear

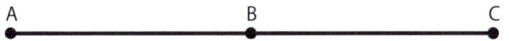

A row of bricks in a wall could be described as being *collinear*, and a line of crows sitting along the top of that wall could also be described as collinear!

column *noun*   عمود

Set of numbers that are vertical in orientation

In arithmetic, addition, subtraction, multiplication and division take place in *columns*, such as hundreds, tens and units. When adding, subtracting, multiplying or dividing, it is very important to write *columns* properly organised by value.

```
  H T U           H T U
  3 7 2           2 7 6
+ 5 6 9         x     3
  -----         -------
  9 4 1           8 2 8
```

common denominator
noun   المقام المشترك

For the fractions: $\frac{1}{2}$ $\frac{2}{3}$ $\frac{5}{6}$ the common denominators of 2, 3 and 6 are the common multiples of 2, 3 and 6; these are 6, 12, 18, 24 …

With *common denominators* of 6, 12, 18, 24 …

$\frac{1}{2}$ $\frac{2}{3}$ $\frac{5}{6}$ can be written as $\frac{3}{6}$ $\frac{4}{6}$ $\frac{5}{6}$

or

$\frac{6}{12}$ $\frac{8}{12}$ $\frac{10}{12}$ or $\frac{9}{18}$ $\frac{12}{18}$ $\frac{15}{18}$

common difference
noun   أساس المتوالية الحسابية / الفرق المشترك

The difference between successive terms in an arithmetic progression (AP)
For example: For the AP, 2, 6, 10, 14, 18, 22, 26 … the *common difference* is +4.

2 6 10 14 18 22 26
+4 +4 +4 +4 +4 +4

A brother and his two sisters were born in the years 1998, 2000 and 2002 – the *common difference* in their ages was 2 years.
See arithmetic progression

common factor
noun   العامل المشترك

A number which is a factor of each number in a group or set
For example:
7 is a *common factor* of 14, 21, 28, 42.

common multiple
noun   المضاعف المشترك

A number which is a multiple of each number in a group or set, for example, 18 and 36 are common multiples of the numbers 2, 6 and 9
30 is a *common multiple* of the numbers 3, 5 and 6.
See LCM

common ratio
noun   أساس المتوالية الهندسية / النسبة المشتركة

The ratio of a term to an immediately prior term in a geometric progression (GP)
For example:

3 6 12 24 48 96 192
x2 x2 x2 x2 x2 x2

For the GP, 3, 6, 12, 24, 48, 96, 192 … the *common ratio* is *x*2.
See geometric progression

compasses

compasses noun
فرجار

Also known as a pair of compasses; a piece of mathematical drawing equipment consisting of two jointed legs, useful for drawing circles; one leg has a pin to stand in place on the paper and the other leg usually has a pencil attached to it for drawing the lines
Jamila used a *compass* to draw a circle of a radius 3 cm.

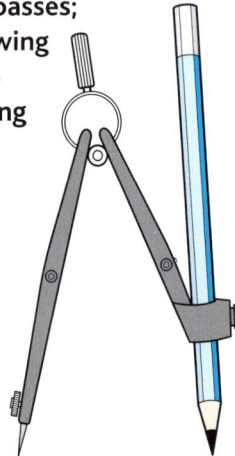

commutative laws
noun
الخاصية التبديلية

The laws for addition and multiplication state that when two or more numbers are added or multiplied the sum or product is the same regardless of the order of the numbers

For example: 2 + 9 = 11   9 + 2 = 11
              4 x 7 = 28   7 x 4 = 28
See associative, distributive laws

complementary angles
noun
زاويتان متتامتان

Complementary angles add up to 1 right angle or 90°
$\angle ABD + \angle DBC = 90°$. $p + q = 90°$.
Compare supplementary angles

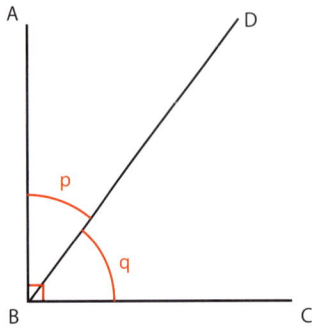

compound interest
noun
ربح مركب

An accumulation of monetary value due to invested capital

An amount of money P is invested at an interest rate of r per cent or $r\%$ per year. After one year, the amount is $P + P(\frac{r}{100})$ or $P(1 + \frac{r}{100})$.
Compounding the interest for the second year the amount is $P(1 + \frac{r}{100})^2$.
After n years the amount is $P(1 + \frac{r}{100})^n$.
If you put your money into a savings account, it will earn more money for you. The amount of money it earns is called the *interest*.
However earning *interest* on your money is not acceptable in some Islamic areas.
See principal

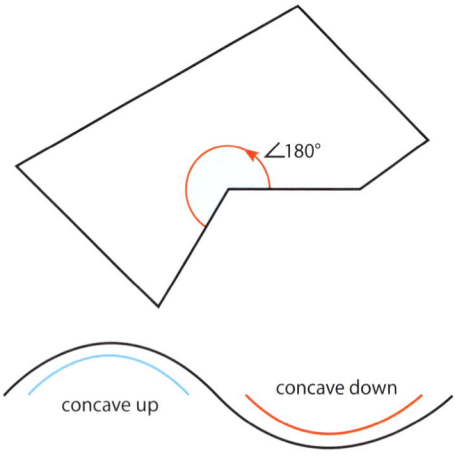

concave adjective
مُقَعَّر

Descriptive of a polygon with an interior angle greater than 180°; descriptive of the inside of a curved region
The inside of a bowl is *concave*.
Compare convex

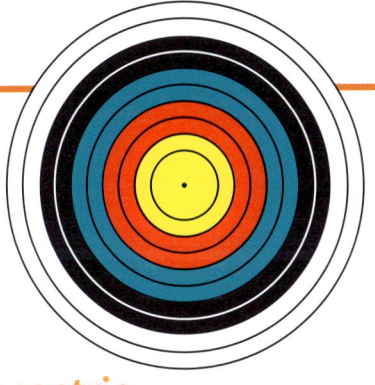

concentric
adjective   دوائر متحدة المركز

Circles which have the same centre are concentric

An archery target is *concentric*, with the centre being the bull's-eye.
See circle

concrete materials
noun   أدوات تعليمية محسوسة

Words meaning 'real objects' used as visual and tactile aids in helping to teach students about number concepts

Pictures of *concrete materials* appear in textbooks to link them to the symbols for numbers and to illustrate the four processes. Some *concrete materials* are particularly useful for teaching young children about the four processes.

counters

Cuisenaire rods

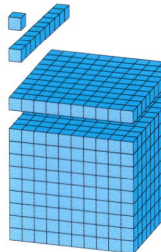
base ten blocks

cone
noun   مخروط

A three-dimensional (3D) solid; it has a circular base and its vertex is directly above the centre of the base

An ice-cream *cone* takes its name from this shape.
See conic sections, vertex

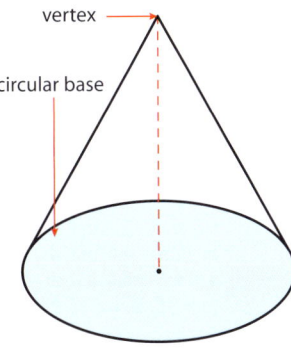

congruent
adjective   متطابقة

Two plane figures are equal in every respect or congruent when one can be placed on the other so as to coincide with all angles and sides

Triangles ABC amd ZXY are congruent.

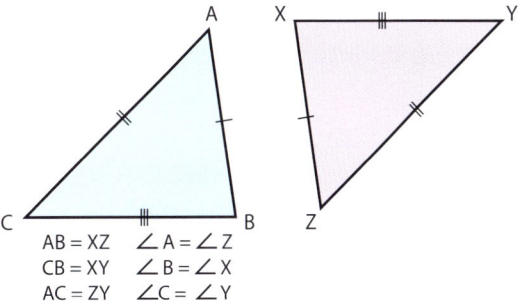

AB = XZ $\angle A = \angle Z$
CB = XY $\angle B = \angle X$
AC = ZY $\angle C = \angle Y$

conic sections
noun   قطوع مخروطية

Cutting a cone produces conic sections

Cutting at an angle to the base of the cone produces an ellipse.

Cutting parallel to the base of the cone produces a circle.

consecutive
adjective   متتالي

Numbers or periods of time which follow each other without interruption

counting numbers: 1 2 3 4 5 6 ...
whole numbers: 0 1 2 3 4 5 6 ...
even numbers: 2 4 6 8 10 ...
days: Mon, Tue, Wed, Thu, Fri, Sat, Sun

If you are given maths homework on Monday, Tuesday and Wednesday, you will have been given maths homework on three *consecutive* days.

15

construct

construct verb   ينشأ / يرسم
Drawing lines, angles and arcs to form figures that have particular shapes and measurements using a ruler, protractor, set-squares and compasses; such instruments make up a geometry set
Khaled *constructed* a right-angled triangle using a protractor and a ruler.

constructions
noun   مخططات / إنشاءات هندسية
Geometric drawings done using compasses, protractors and other drawing instruments found in a geometry set
Construction drawing is one aspect of daughtmanship in the preparation of plans for buildings and bridges. It can be found on architectual and civil engineering plans.

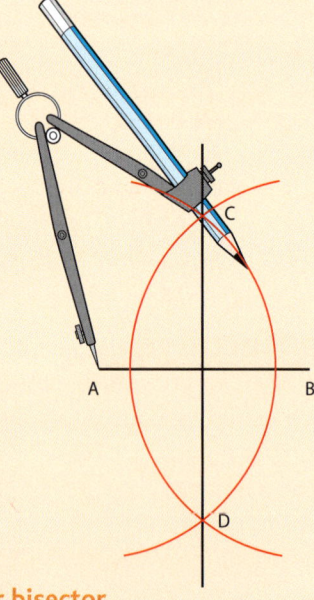

perpendicular bisector
Centre A, radius > ½ AB, draw an arc above and below AB. Centre B, same radius, draw arcs to cut the previous arcs at C and D. Join CD. CD is the perpendicular bisector of AB.

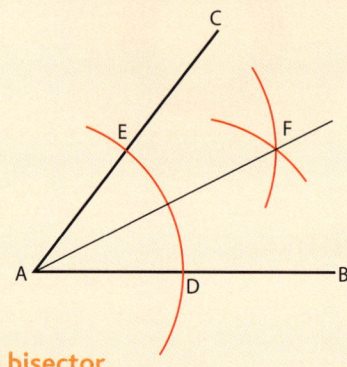

angle bisector
Draw any angle BAC. Centre A, any radius, draw an arc to cut AB and AC at D and E. Centres D and E, same radius, draw arcs to cut at F. Join AF. AF is the bisector of ∠ BAC.

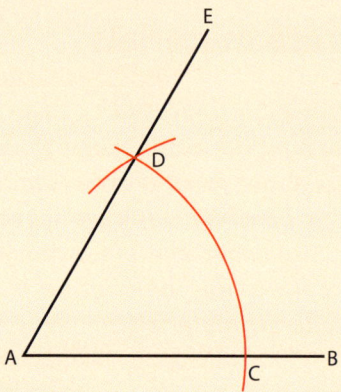

an angle of 60°
Draw AB. Centre A, any radius, draw an arc to cut AB at C. Centre C, same radius, draw an to cut the previous arc at D. Join AD and produce to E. ∠ BAE = 60°.

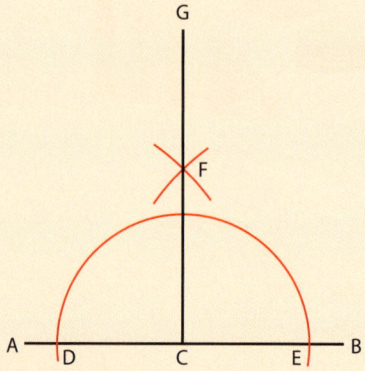

an angle of 90°
Draw AB. Centre C, any point on AB, draw arcs on AB on either side of C at D and E. Centres D and E, radius > ½ DE, draw arcs to cut at F. Join CF and produce to G. ∠ BCG = ∠ ACG = 90°.

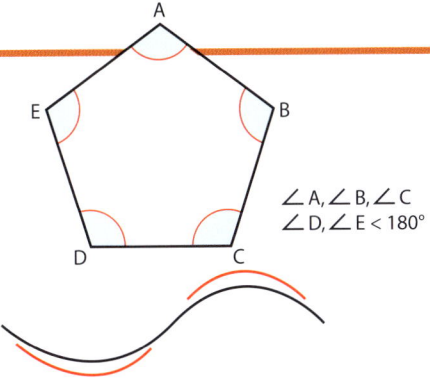

convex *adjective*   محدب
Descriptive of a polygon with no interior angle greater than 180° descriptive of the outside of a curved region
While the inside of a bowl or a cup is concave, the outside is *convex*.
Compare concave

coordinates
noun   إحداثيات
A pair of values that identify a position on a flat surface; the two values are known as the '*x*' and '*y*' coordinates
The *coordinates* of A are (4, 7). The '*x*' *coordinate* of A is 4 and its '*y*' *coordinate* is 7. The '*x*' *coordinate* is always given first.
See axis

cross-multiply *verb*   ضرب تبادلي
A technique for simplifying an equation which has fractions
For example:

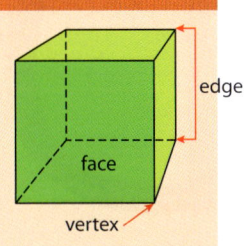
cross-multiply

The same result can also be obtained by multiplying both sides of the equation by the lowest multiple of the denominators.

cylinder

cube *noun*   مكعب
A three-dimensional (3D) solid that has 6 square faces, 12 edges and 8 corners or vertices
A *cube* can also be called a hexahedron, meaning a solid with 6 faces.
Hex- is the prefix for 6.
An ice-*cube* probably originally got its name from its shape.
Standard dice and Rubik's cubes are good examples of *cubes*.
See polyhedron, solid or 3D shapes

cuboid *noun*   متوازي مستطيلات
A 3D solid with 6 rectangular faces, 12 edges and 8 vertices; opposite faces are congruent
A *cuboid* can also be called a rectangular prism.
See prism, solids or 3D shapes

cylinder *noun*   أسطوانة
A 3D solid with 3 faces, 2 edges and 0 vertices; the two circular faces are at right angles to the curved surface
You can often find *cylindrical* (adjective) storage jars in kitchens.
A *cylinder* can also be called a circular prism.
See prism, solid or 3D shapes

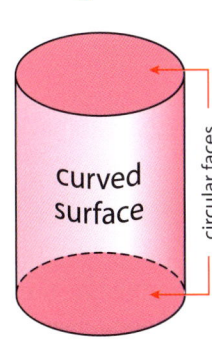

17

Dd

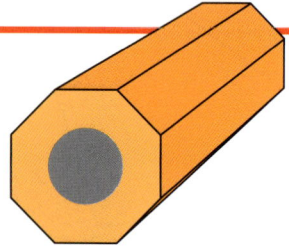

decahedron
noun   مجسم معشَّر السّطوح / ذو عشرة أوجه
A polyhedron with ten faces
This unsharpened pencil is a *decahedron*. It is also called an octagonal prism.
See polyhedron, prism, solid or 3D shapes

Months	Jan	Feb	Mar	Apr	May	Jun	July	Aug	Sept	Oct	Nov	Dec
Max °C	22	25	29	33	38	44	45	44	40	34	27	22
Min °C	7	10	13	17	22	28	29	29	26	20	13	8

Sahara desert temperatures

data   *noun*   بيانات
A collection of facts, numbers or symbols; data or information can be stored in a database on a computer or, when appropriate, in a table of values
The above *data* is the result of a survey to find the maximum and minimum temperatures in the Sahara desert over one year. It could also be recorded on a graph.
See graphs

decagon
noun   مضلع عشاري / ذو عشرة أضلاع
A polygon with ten sides; deca- is a prefix meaning 10

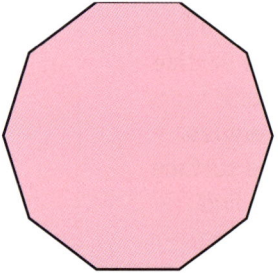

In athletics, the *decathlon* involves 10 different events.
See plane or 2D shapes, polygon

decimal   *noun/adjective*   عشري
Relating to grouping in tens or a base of 10; fractions with denominators of 10, 100, 1000 ... can be written as decimals: 0.1, 0.01, 0.001 ...
Numbers in base 10 are grouped in ones, tens, hundreds ... or 1, 10, 100, 1000... or $10^0, 10^1, 10^2, 10^3$ ...
Note that:
$100 = 10 \times 10 = 10^1 \times 10^1 = 10^{1+1} = 10^2$

and $\dfrac{1}{100} = \dfrac{1}{10 \times 10} = \dfrac{1}{10} \times \dfrac{1}{10}$

$= 10^{-1} \times 10^{-1} = 10^{(-1) + (-1)} = 10^{-2}$

See base, denominator

deci-   *prefix*   ديسي: بادئة بمعنى عُشرْ
Metric system prefix for $\frac{1}{10}$
10 centimetres = 1 decimetre   10 cm = 1 dm
10 decimetres = 1 metre   10 dm = 1 m

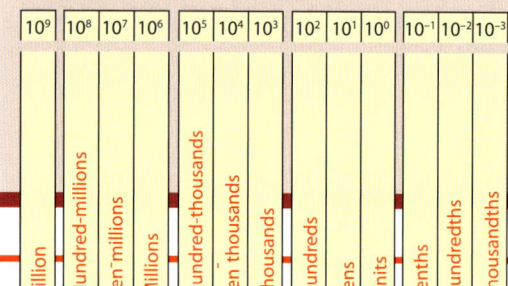

diameter

decrease verb   ينقص
To subtract from a value

For example:
8 - 5 = 3

8 is decreased by 5
5 is subtracted from 8
5 is deducted from 8

In the subtraction sentence, 8 - 5 = 3:
5 is the subtrahend, 8 is the minuend and 3 is the difference.
If there are five apples in a bowl and 2 of them get eaten, the number of apples in the bowl has *decreased* by 2.
See subtraction

degree noun   درجة
Degree (°) is the unit for the measurement of angles
On a rectangular table, the sides meet at angles of 90 degrees.
See angle

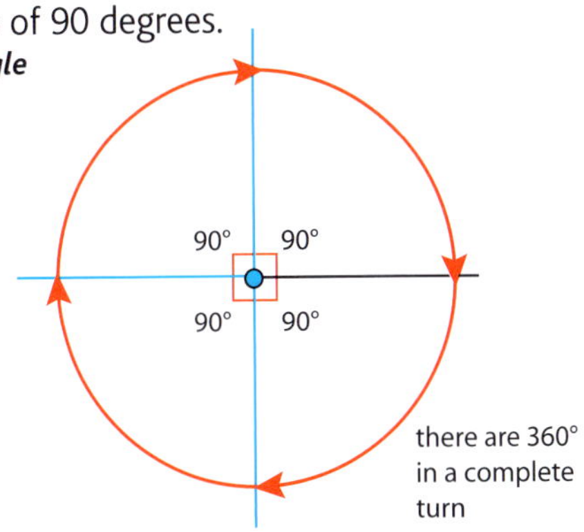

90° 90°
90° 90°

there are 360°
in a complete turn

denominator noun   مقام الكسر
Proper fractions have two parts – a numerator and a denominator; the denominator is the total number of parts
See fraction

descending adjective   تنازلي
Descending literally means 'going down' and in mathematics refers to the order within a group of values
A group of values in *descending* order is listed from largest to smallest. For example, if you were to list the numbers 4, 16, 2, 8, 19, 33 in *descending* order, you would have 33, 19, 16, 8, 4, 2.
See ascending

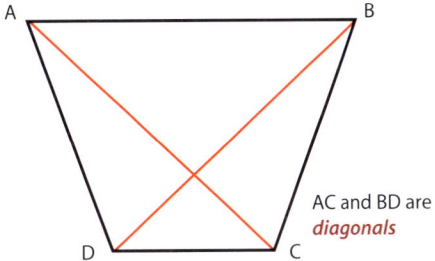

AC and BD are *diagonals*

diagonal noun   قطري
A straight line joining non-adjacent vertices
When a television or computer screen measurement is given, that measurement is always taken on the *diagonal*.
A triangle has no *diagonals*.

diameter noun   قطر الدائرة
A diameter of a circle is a straight line passing through its centre from arc to arc; it divides the circle into two semicircles 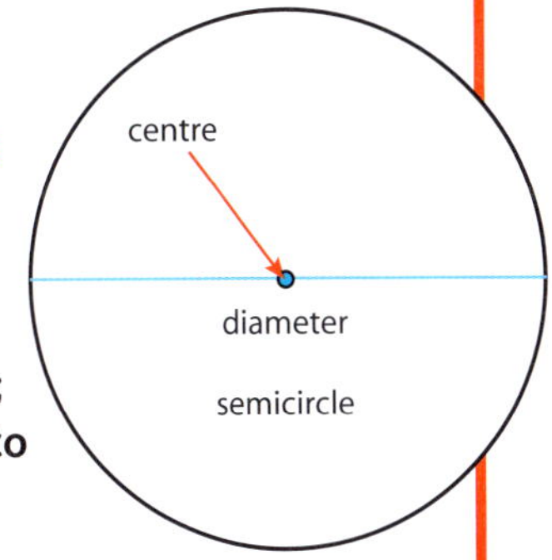
If a circular table is described as being 1.5 m across the length of its *diameter* is 1.5 m.
See circle

19

difference

difference noun   الفرق
The number which results from a subtraction calculation
For example, in the subtraction sentence
19 – 8 = 11 the *difference* is 11.
See minuend, subtraction, subtrahend

digit noun   رقم
Any of the ten Hindu-Arabic numerals 0, 1, 2, 3, 4, 5, 6, 7, 8, 9 used to write all numbers in the base 10 system
10 486 is a 5-*digit* number.
5 364 291 is a 7-*digit* number.

digital adjective   رقمي
Anything that uses digits to provide information can be described as digital
A *digital* clock displays the time by showing numbers, unlike an analogue clock, which uses hands to point.
A *digital* thermometer displays the temperature using numbers, rather than using mercury and a scale marked on the side of the thermometer.
See analogue

dimension   بُعد
Reference to the length, width and height of entities or objects
A line or curve is described as one-*dimensional* (1D) having length only.
2D shapes or flat shapes have the *dimensions* of length and width such as polygons and circles.
3D shapes or solid shapes have the *dimensions* of length, width and height such as polyhedra and prisms.
See circle, plane or 2D shapes, polygon, polyhedron, solid or 3D shapes

direct proportion noun   تناسب طردي
Relation between two variable quantities a and b, such as a = kb, where k is a constant
For example: if *a* stands for the fuel used by a generator in an hour, *b* the hours it runs and *k* = 0.5; how many litres of fuel will the generator use in a day?
a = kb   a = 0.5 x 24   a = 12 litres
See indirect proportion, proportion

directed number
noun   الأعداد الموجّهة / الأعداد الموجبة والسالبة
An integer or signed number
Numbers besides zero can have a positive or negative sign for example +5 or -5, although when a number has no sign, it is understood to be positive.
Integers can be positive, negative or 0.
This number line shows *directed numbers* from -7 to 7.

-7 -6 -5 -4 -3 -2 -1   0 +1 +2 +3 +4 +5 +6 +7

The opposite or inverse of 7 is -7.
The sum of all inverse integers is 0.
7 + (-7) = 0
See integer

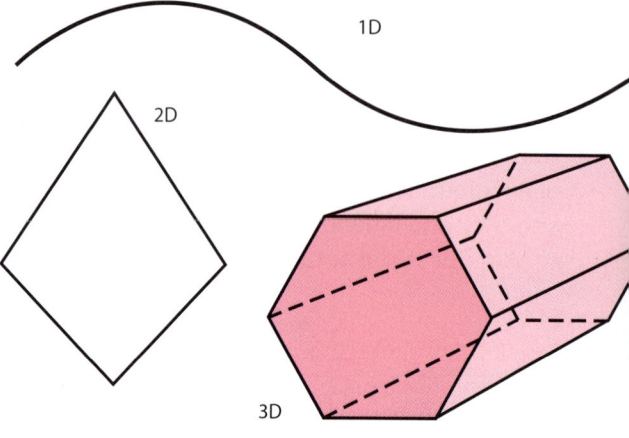

1D
2D
3D

20

dividend

direction noun   اتجاه
Position relative to the points of the compass
The bearing of objects such as ships and aircraft also indicate *direction*.
Bearings are angles, expressed in 3 digits as the amount of turn, clockwise from the North.

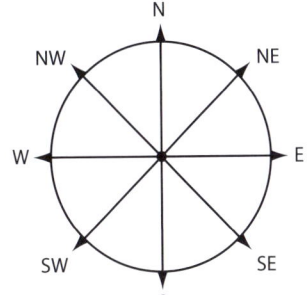

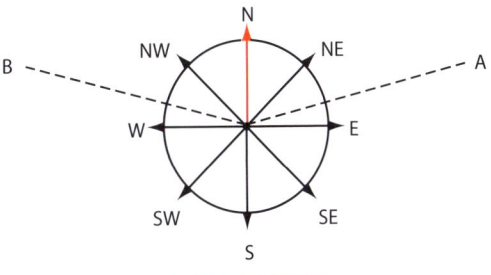

Bearing A = 071°.
Bearing B = 278°.

disjoint set noun   مجموعات منفصلة
Two sets, A and B, are disjoint if they do not have any elements, or members, in common
This is denoted by:
A = {1, 3, 5, 7}
B = {2, 4, 6, 8}
A ξ B = ∅

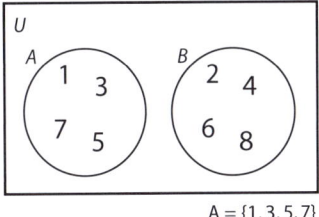

A = {1, 3, 5, 7}
B = {2, 4, 6, 8}

This means that there are no elements, or members, at the intersection of sets A and B. Two school year groups are *disjointed sets* beacuse no student can be in both years at once.
See intersection, union of sets

distributive law
noun   الخاصية التوزيعية
In 5 x (3 + 4) the '5 x' is distributed across the (3 + 4) to form 5 groups of 3 and 5 groups of 4
5 x (3 + 4) = 5 x 3 + 5 x 4
= 15 + 20
= 35
See associative, commutative laws

dividend noun   المقسوم
The number which is being divided in a division sentence
In 10 ÷ 5 = 2, 10 is the *dividend*.
See division

division

division noun   القسمة
Division is:
- finding out how many groups are contained in a value;
- sharing a value into equal groups;
- the inverse of multiplication

In the *division* sentence 28 ÷ 4 = 7
28 is the dividend, 4 is the divisor and 7 is the quotient.
Farida used *division* to work out that if she had 20 sweets, and 4 friends to share them with, Fardia and her friends would get 4 sweets each.
See associative, commutative laws, signs

duodecimal
adjective   نظام الترقيم الاثنا عشري
Relating to a number system with a base of 12. The base 12 system uses 12 digits: 0, 1, 2, 3, 4, 5, 6, 7, 8, 9, T (for ten), E (for eleven. 12 is written 10 meaning one twelve, zero ones or units

Duodecimal 100 or 100 $_{\text{base 12}}$
= (1 x 12^2) + (0 x 12^1) + (0 x 12^0) $_{\text{base 10}}$
= (144   +   0   +   0) $_{\text{base 10}}$
= 144 $_{\text{base 10}}$
See base, decimal

dodecagon noun
مضلع اثنا عشري / ذو اثني عشر ضلعًا
A polygon with 12 sides; a dodecagon, like other polygons, can be regular or irregular
Dodeca- is a prefix meaning 12.
See plane or 2D shapes, polygon

Regular *dodecagon*

Irregular *dodecagon*

dodecahedron
noun   مجسم ذو اثني عشر وجهًا
A polyhedron with twelve faces
This regular *dodecahedron* has twelve pentagonal faces. A decagonal prism is also a dodecahedron.
See prism, polyhedron, solid or 3D shapes

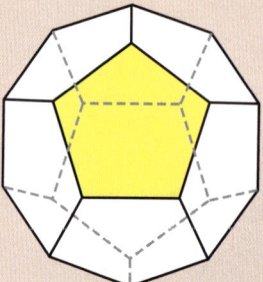
Regular *dodecahedron*

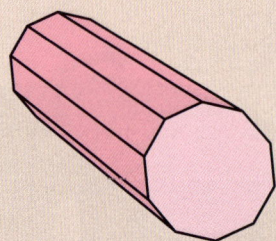
decagonal prism

Ee

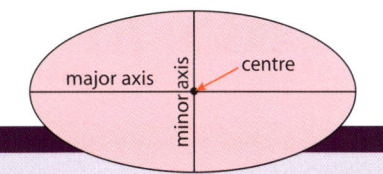

ellipse *noun* شكل بيضاوي
A closed 2D figure which can be described as an elongated circle
The *ellipse* is symmetrical about two axes – a minor axis and major axis.
See conic sections

ellipsoid *noun* مجسم بيضاوي
A 3D shape which is symmetrical about three axes
The three sections of the *ellipsoid* are ellipses or circles.
See conic section

edge *noun* حرف / حافة المجسم
The faces of solid (3D) shapes, apart from the sphere and ellipsoid, meet at an edge
A cuboid has twelve *edges*.
A cone has one *edge*.
Cut diamonds have many *edges*.
See cone, conic section, cuboid

empty set *noun* مجموعة فارغة
A set that has no elements, or members, is called an empty or null set; the empty set is denoted by Ø
For example:
E = {even numbers ending in 1}
E = Ø, then: nE = 0 (number of elements = 0)
P = {prime numbers with three factors}
P = Ø, then: nP = 0
see null set

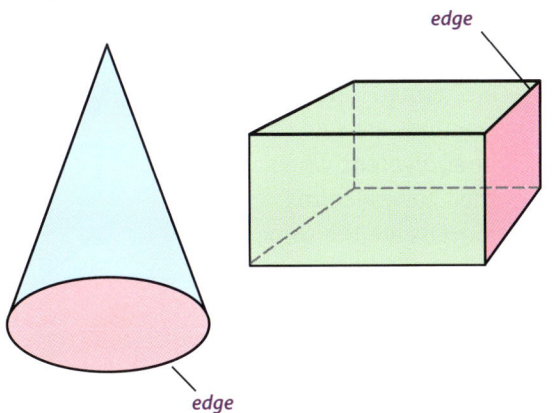
edge

23

equals sign

equals sign noun إشارة المساواة
The name for the twin lines symbol (=) meaning 'is equal to'; it is used to show that two things are the same size, number or amount
For example: 1000 g = 1 kg

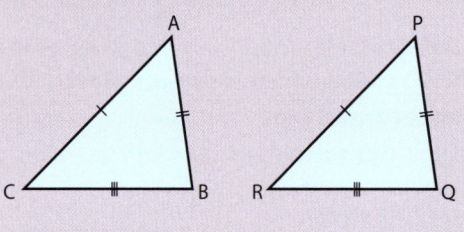

AB = PQ   BC = QR   AC = PR

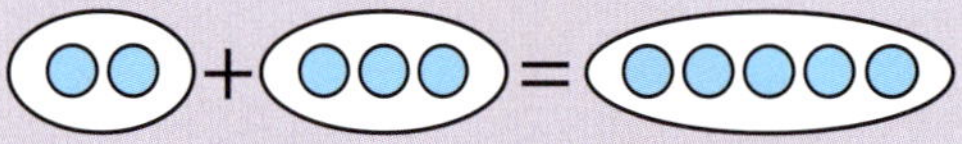

2 + 3 = 5

see signs

equation noun معادلة
A statement that shows that quantities are equal; an equation has two sides and an 'equals' sign (=) between them
Adding the same number to, or subtracting the same number from, each side of the *equation* can lead to evaluating the unknown.
For example:

$a + 5 = 9$	$b - 4 = 3$
$a + 5 - 5 = 9 - 5$	$b - 4 + 4 = 3 + 4$
$a = 4$	$b = 7$

Multiplying or dividing each side of the *equation* by the same number can lead to evaluating the unknown.

$c \times \frac{1}{2} = 3$	$5 \times d = 25$
$c \times \frac{1}{2} \times 2 = 3 \times 2$	$5 \div 5 \times d = 25 \div 5$
$c = 6$	$d = 5$

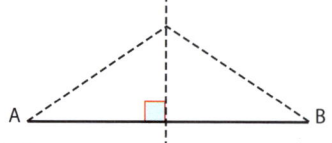

equidistant adjective متساوي البعد (عن نقطة معينة)
Being the same distance from a given position or point
All points on the perpendicular bisector of a line AB are *equidistant* from A and B.

equilateral adjective تساوي الأضلاع
Having equal sides; regular polygons have equal sides and equal angles
For example:

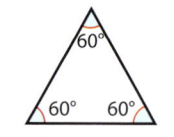
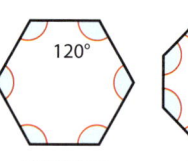

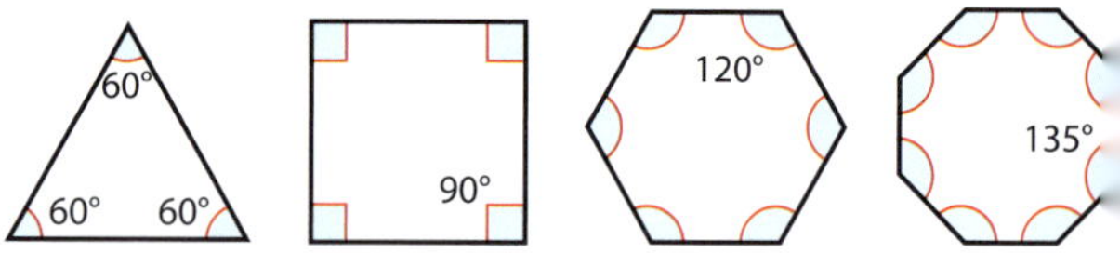

equilateral triangle   square   pentagon   hexagon

See plane or 2D shapes, polygon

equivalent adjective متساوي / متكافئ
A term to describe two things which are equal
If the angles in two triangles are *equivalent* (equal) then the triangles are termed 'similar'.
Fractions are said to be *equivalent* when their 'lowest terms' formats are the same.

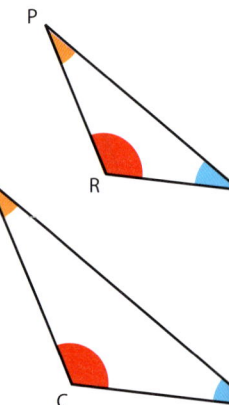

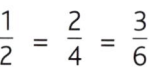

$\frac{1}{2} = \frac{2}{4} = \frac{3}{6}$

See fraction, similar triangles

exterior angle

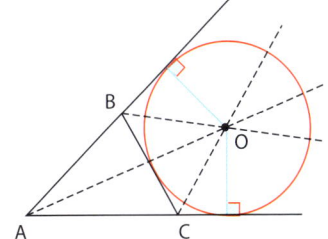

escribed circle noun   دائرة تمس أضلاع المثلث من الخارج
The circle, centre O, is an escribed circle of triangle ABC
O is located at the intersection of the bisectors of interior ∠ A, exterior ∠ B and exterior ∠ C.
AB and AC extended, with BC, are tangents to the *escribed circle*.
See exterior angle, tangent

even number noun   عدد زوجي
All even numbers are divisible by 2 and end in 0, 2, 4, 6 or 8
For example: 25 654 is an even number.
Tariq has an *even number* of brothers and sisters; he has four.

event noun   حدث
In probability, an experiment or trial such as tossing a coin or rolling a die
The calculation for the probability of the result being a six in a die rolling *event* is given by:

Probability = $\frac{\text{Number of events showing six}}{\text{Total number of events}}$

See probability

expanded notation
noun   الصورة المطوّلة (المُوسَّعة) للعدد
Shows the value of each digit, in numbers, in any base
For example:
$365_{\text{base 10}}$ = (3 × 100) + (6 × 10) + (5 × 1)
= (3 × 10^2) + (6 × 10^1) + (5 × 10^0)

$101_{\text{base 2}}$ = (1 × 4) + (0 × 2) + (1 × 1)
= (1 × 2^2) + (0 × 2^1) + (1 × 2^0)

See base, digit

exponent noun   الأس
Another term for index or power
For example, in 4^5, 5 is the *exponent*.
4^5 is another way of writing 4 × 4 × 4 × 4 × 4.
See index

extension noun   امتداد
Literally, an added piece
If you want to measure an exterior angle on any polygon, you need to extend one side of the polygon. This extra line is the *extension*.

exterior angle
noun   زاوية خارجية
An angle of a polygon formed at the extension of a side and an adjacent side

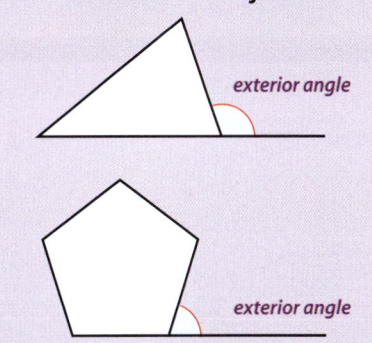

25

factor noun   عامل / قاسم

In arithmetic, a whole number that a number is divisible by

1 is a *factor* of all numbers.
All numbers are *factors* of themselves.
Numbers whose only *factors* are themselves and 1 are prime numbers.

Divisibility checks	
12 ÷ **1** = 12	1
12 ÷ **2** = 6	2
12 ÷ **3** = 4	3
12 ÷ **4** = 3	4
12 ÷ **6** = 2	6
12 ÷ **12** = 1	12

In algebra, the term $5pq$ has eight *factors*:

$1, 5, p, q, 5p, 5q, pq, 5pq$

$5y$ is a common *factor* for the terms in the expression $5y^2 - 10y$.
The expression can be *factorised* by dividing each term by $5y$: $5y^2 - 10y = 5y(y - 2)$.
See common factor, prime number

finite adjective   محدود / منتهي

Having a limit

Set A of even whole numbers up to 100 is a *finite* set. Set A = {0, 2, 4, 6 ... 100}
Set B of even whole numbers is an infinite set. Set B = {0, 2, 4, 6 ...}
See infinite, infinity

flat adjective   مسطح

2D (two-dimensional) shapes are flat shapes; their dimensions are length and width; triangles, squares, rectangles and circles are flat or 2D shapes

Hundreds of years ago, before scientists discovered that the Earth was round, sailors used to believe that it was *flat*.
Non-*flat* shapes are called solids or 3D shapes. Solid shapes with triangle, square, rectangle or circular faces are called prisms.
See plane or 2D shapes, prism, solid or 3D shapes

figure noun   رقم

A numeral

A two-digit number, such as 25, is said to have double *figures*.
1 million (1 000 000) is a 7-*figure* number.

figure noun   شكل

A shape

A square can be described as a four-sided *figure*. A cube can be described as a *figure* with six faces.
See digit

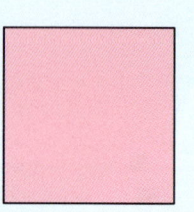
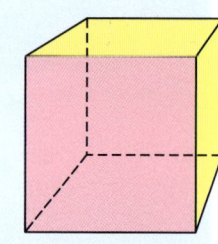

formula

formula *noun* قانون / قاعدة

Numbers or letters that represent a rule

In geometry, ***formulae*** are used to calculate the dimensions of 2D and 3D shapes. For example, the area of a rectangle is calculated by multiplying its length by its width (or breadth). The ***formula*** for calculating the area of a rectangle is expressed in the equation:

$A = L \times W$.

'L' represents the length, 'W' represents the width and 'A' represents the area. The ***formula*** for the perimeter of a rectangle is: $P = 2l + 2w$ or $P = 2(l + w)$.

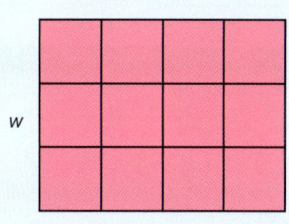

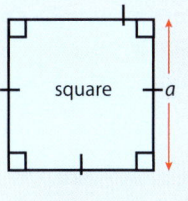

w
l

square
a

perimeter = $4a$
area = a^2

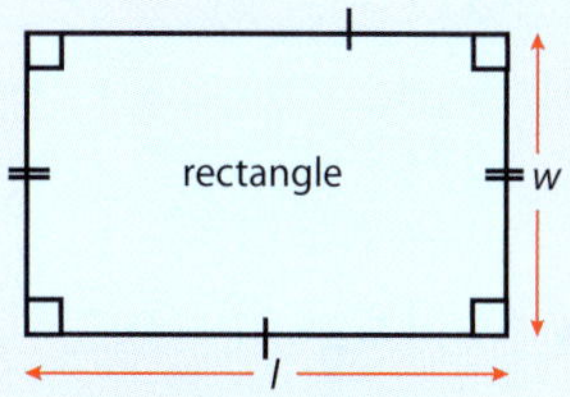

rectangle
w
l

perimeter = $2(l \times w)$
area = $l \times w$

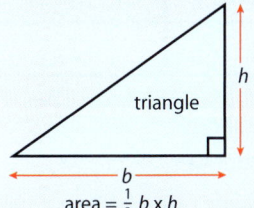

triangle
h
b

area = $\frac{1}{2}\, b \times h$

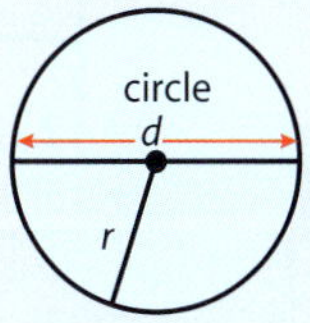

circle
d
r

area = πr^2
circumference = $2\pi r$

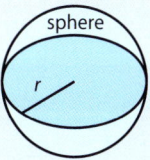

sphere
r

volume = $\frac{4}{3}\pi r^3$
surface area = $4\pi r^2$

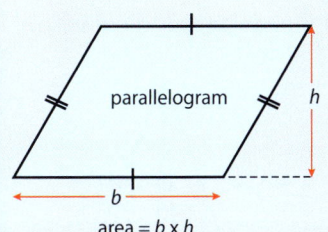

parallelogram
h
b

area = $b \times h$

r
cylinder
h

volume = $\pi r^2 h$
surface area = $2\pi rh$

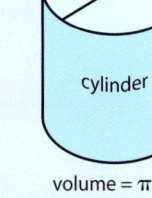

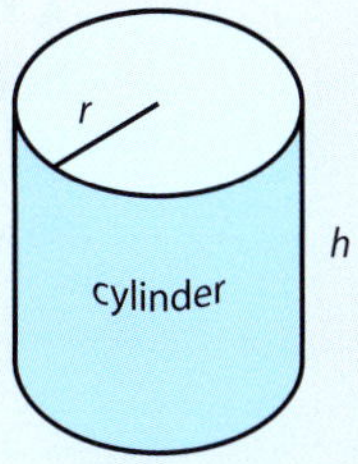

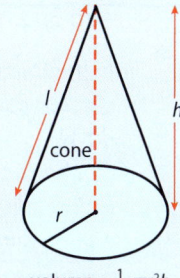

l
h
cone
r

volume = $\frac{1}{3}\pi r^2 h$
surface area = πrl

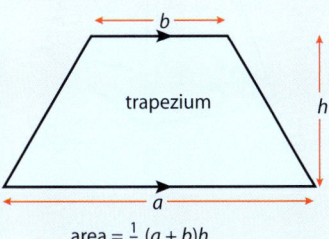

b
trapezium
h
a

area = $\frac{1}{2}(a + b)h$

a
cube
a
a

volume = a^3
surface area = $6a^2$

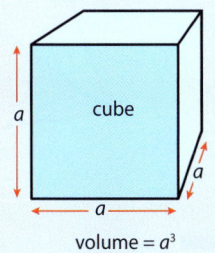

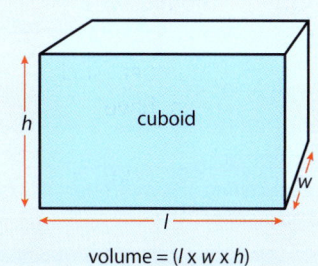

h
cuboid
w
l

volume = $(l \times w \times h)$
total area = $2(lh + wh + lw)$

fraction

fraction noun   كسر
A fraction is written as the ratio of two integers known as the numerator and denominator

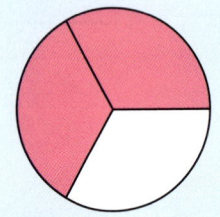
Numerator → 2
Denominator → 3
means 2 out of 3 equal parts

1 whole					
$\frac{1}{3}$		$\frac{1}{3}$		$\frac{1}{3}$	
$\frac{1}{6}$	$\frac{1}{6}$	$\frac{1}{6}$	$\frac{1}{6}$	$\frac{1}{6}$	$\frac{1}{6}$

$\frac{2}{3}$ and $\frac{4}{6}$ are equivalent *fractions*

$\frac{2}{3}$ and $\frac{4}{6}$ are simple *fractions*

In simple or common *fractions* the denominator is always greater than the numerator.

$\frac{3}{2}$ and $\frac{6}{4}$ are vulgar or improper *fractions*

In vulgar or improper *fractions* the denominator is always less than the numerator.
See cancelling, decimal, improper fraction, mixed number

frequency noun   تكرار
How many times an item appears in gathered information or data
For example:
How often did each of the vowels appear in a 29-word paragraph? The vowels were tallied.

vowels	tally	frequency
a	ℍℍ ℍℍ ‖‖	13
e	ℍℍ ℍℍ ‖‖‖‖	14
i	ℍℍ ℍℍ ℍℍ	15
o	ℍℍ ℍℍ ‖	12
u	‖	2

'i' has the highest *frequency*
'u' has the lowest *frequency*
See data, tally

frustum   مجسم ناقص (الجزء العلوي)
A frustum of a pyramid is the section between parallel planes perpendicular to its axis

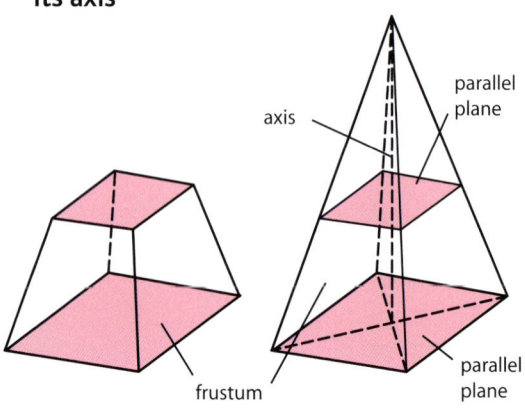

geometric progression (GP)
noun   المتوالية الهندسية

A sequence of terms, in which the ratio of each term to the preceding term is constant

This constant is known as the common ratio. For example in the series: 3, 6, 12, 24, 48, the common ratio between each pair is:

$$\frac{6}{3}=2 \quad \frac{12}{6}=2 \quad \frac{24}{12}=2 \quad \frac{48}{24}=2\ldots$$

The common ratio between each term and the next is × 2. So the 6th term will be 96.

Calculating the 6th and 7th terms:
6th term = 5th term × common ratio
           48 × 2 = 96
7th term = 96 × 2 = 192
Compare arithmetic progression, common ratio

geometry
noun   الهندسة

The study of the relationships between the:
- **sides, angles and vertices in flat or 2D shapes;**
- **surfaces, edges and vertices in solid or 3D shapes**

See angle, vertex, polygon, polyhedron

giga- *prefix*   جيجا: بادئة بمعنى ألف مليون

Prefix for multiples of a billion (thousand million) or 10^9 in units of the metric system

Computer memory is now often measured in *giga*bytes (GB).
1 *giga*byte = 1000 megabytes
See metric and SI units

gradient

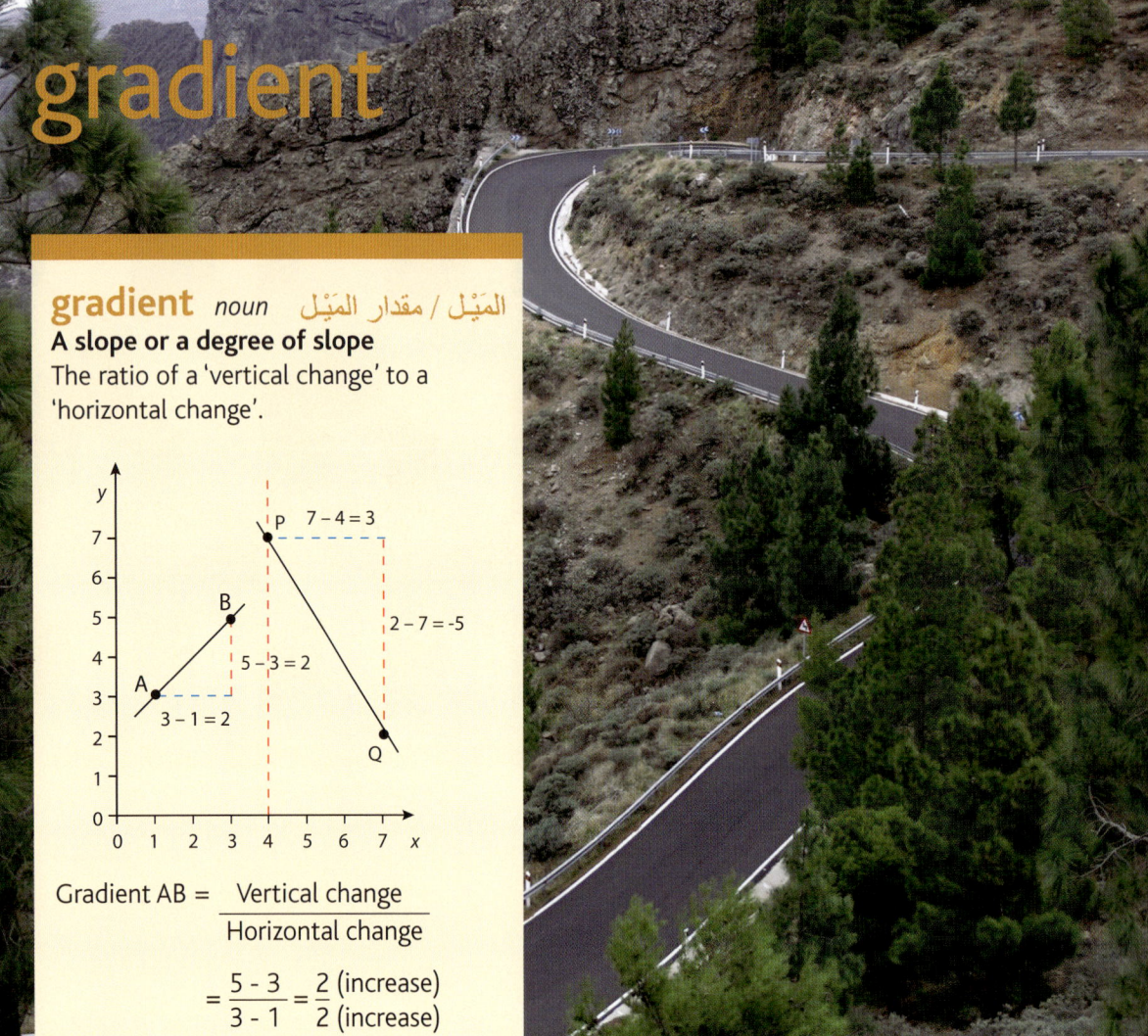

gradient noun   المَيْل / مقدار المَيْل

A slope or a degree of slope
The ratio of a 'vertical change' to a 'horizontal change'.

Gradient AB = $\dfrac{\text{Vertical change}}{\text{Horizontal change}}$

$= \dfrac{5-3}{3-1} = \dfrac{2 \text{ (increase)}}{2 \text{ (increase)}}$

$= 1$

AB has a positive *gradient* – upwards from left to right.

Gradient PQ = $\dfrac{\text{Vertical change}}{\text{Horizontal change}}$

$= \dfrac{2-7}{7-4} = \dfrac{-5 \text{ (decrease)}}{3 \text{ (increase)}}$

$= 1\tfrac{2}{3}$

PQ has a negative *gradient* – downwards from left to right.
On steeply-sloping roads there are often road signs telling drivers how steep the *gradient* of the road is.
see slope

gram noun   جرام / غرام
Metric unit of mass
Alternative spelling – gramme
Symbol: g
1000 g = 1 kilogram (kg)
1 cubic centimetre (cm^3) of water weighs 1 g
1 millilitre (ml) of water weighs 1 g
In cookery books, the amounts of ingredients needed for a recipe are given in *grams*.
See metric and SI units

graphs

graphs noun   رسم بياني / بيان

A presentation of pictures, bars, straight lines, circles and curves to show how two sets of values are related; the various forms of graph are called, bar charts, pictographs, pie charts, histograms and line graphs; the type of graph you choose to use depends partly on the information that you want to display

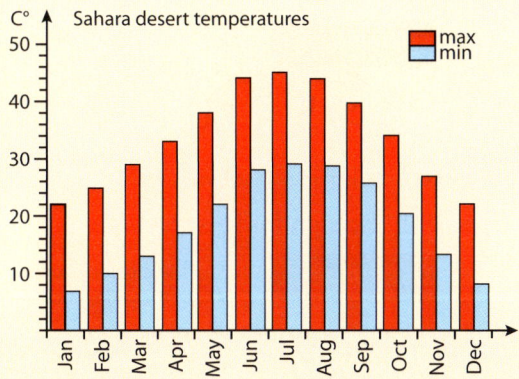

bar chart   رسم بياني بالأعمدة / مخطط أعمدة

This vertical bar chart shows the maximum and minimum temperatures in the Sahara desert over the period of a year.

Bar charts can also be presented horizontally, as with this bar chart which shows the results of a survey of students' tastes in television programmes.

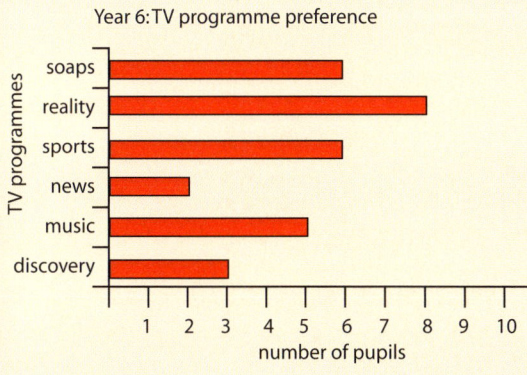

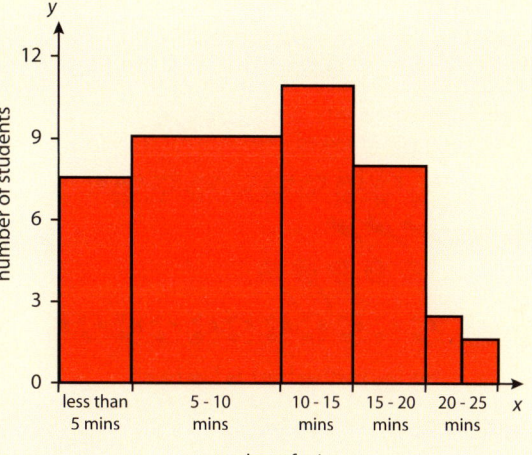

histogram   مدرج تكراري

The *histogram* above shows how long it took students to travel to school. The x axis indicates the number of students, the y axis indicates the amount of time it took them to travel.

line graph   التمثيل بالخط البياني

The annual total number of students in a school were recorded in a *line graph* to show the school's rate of growth.

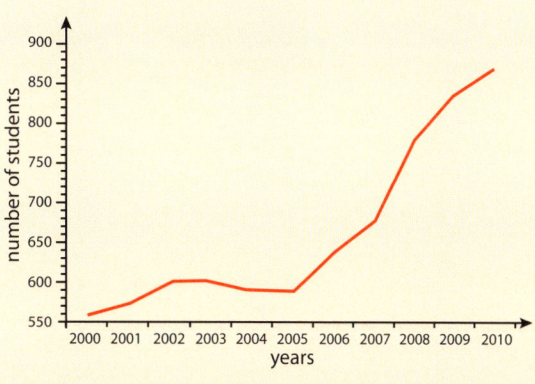

31

graphs

pictograph   المصوّرات

The students in Class 3 were asked what their favourite sport was, and their answers were recorded in a *pictograph*.

Class 3: favourite sports
Key: 1 picture = 2 children

pie chart   التمثيل البياني بالقطاعات الدائرية

Class 4: favourite colours.
Key: 10° = 1 child

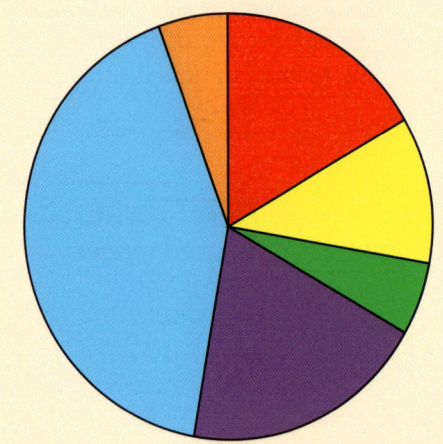

See frequency, tally

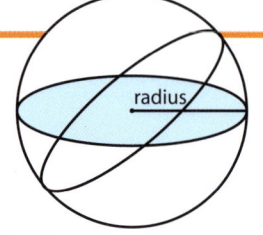

great circle
noun   الدائرة العظمى (في الكرة)

A circular section of a sphere with its centre at the centre of the sphere

If you cut a cricket ball in exactly half the flat surface you are left with is a *great circle*.

greater / less than
sign   أكبر / أقل من

The sign for greater than is >

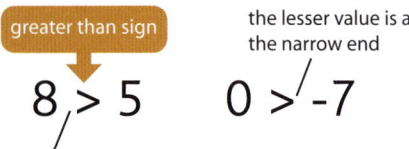

the greater value is at the wider end

Opposite: The sign for less than is <

the lesser value is at the narrow end

greatest common factor (GCF)
noun   العامل المشترك الأكبر

The greatest number which divides exactly into two or more numbers

Example: GCF of 35, 56 and 84
           35 = 5 x 7
           56 = 8 x 7 = 2 x 2 x 2 x 7
           84 = 12 x 7 = 2 x 2 x 3 x 7

5, 8 and 12 are not common factors

7 is a common factor and the *GCF*.

GCF of 35, 56 and 84 = 7

GCF is also known as greatest common divisor (GCD) and highest common factor (HCF). The *GCF* is used to reduce fractions to their lowest terms.

See common factor, highest common factor

Hh

hectare *noun* هكتار
The area of a square which has sides of 100 metres (m) each
1 *hectare* (ha) = 10 000 square metres (m²).
1 are (a) = $\frac{1}{100}$ ha.
The size of a nature reserve is often measured in hectares.
See are

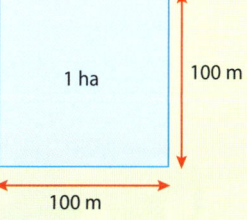

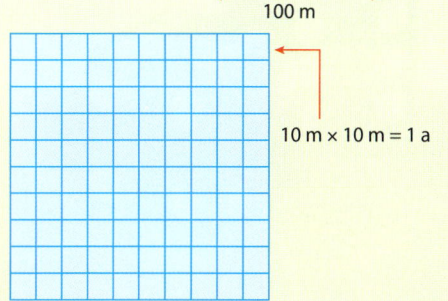

hecto- or hect-
prefix هكتو: بادئة بمعنى مائة
Metric system prefix for 100
A *hectare* is 100 ares; and, although rarely used:
1 *hecto*gram = 100 grams
1 *hecto*litre = 100 litres
1 *hecto*metre = 100 metres
See metric and SI units

-hedron
suffix هيدرون: مقطع يدل على مجسم
Suffix denoting a polyhedron
Examples:
tetrahedron – four surfaces
octahedron – eight surfaces
decahedron – ten surfaces
dodecahedron – twelve surfaces
See polyhedron, solid or 3D shapes

height *noun* ارتفاع
In mathematics an alternative term for the altitude of a polygon; the length of any straight line from a vertex that is perpendicular to an opposite side or a side produced
For example:

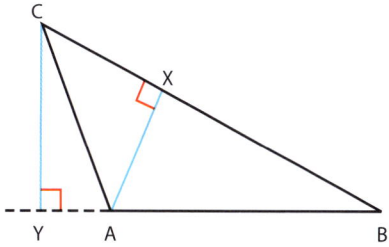

AX is a height for △ ABC. It is a straight line from vertex A and perpendicular to side BC. CY is a height for △ ABC. It is a straight line from vertex C and perpendicular to side BA produced.
See altitude

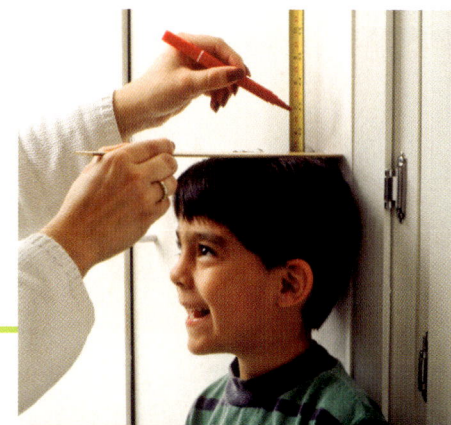

33

hemisphere

hemisphere *noun*   نصف كرة
Hemi- is the prefix for a half; a hemisphere is half a sphere; it has a circular plane and all points on its curved surface are equidistant from its centre
New Zealand is in the southern *hemisphere*; Canada is in the northern *hemisphere*.
See sphere

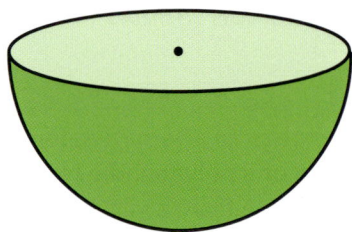

hepta- *prefix*   هبتا: بادئة بمعنى سباعي
Prefix denoting seven
A *heptagon* has seven sides and a *heptahedron* has seven faces.

hexagon *noun*   سداسي
A polygon with six sides
Some types of wire mesh are made up of masses of joined hexagons and honeycombs are also made up of thousands of tiny *hexagons* joined together.
See plane or 2D shapes, polygon

hexadecimal
noun   نظام الترقيم السادس عشري
A number system with a base of sixteen; it has sixteen digits: 0, 1, 2, 3, 4, 5, 6, 7, 8, 9, A, B, C, D, E, F, where A to F stand for the numbers 10 to 15 in base ten; 10 in hexadecimal represents 1 sixteen, 0 ones or units
The *hexadecimal* system is sometimes used by computer programmers.
See base

hexahedron
noun   مجسم سداسي السطوح
A polyhedron with six faces
A die is an example of a *hexahedron*.
See polyhedron, solid or 3D shapes

hypotenuse

highest common factor
noun   العامل المشترك الأعلى
See greatest common factor

histogram *noun*   مدرّج تكراري
A column graph with no spaces between the columns
See bar chart, graphs

horizontal *adjective*   أفقي
Literally, relating to or parallel to the horizon

A graph's '*x*-axis' is the *horizontal* axis. It is at right angles or perpendicular to the vertical '*y*-axis'.
See axis

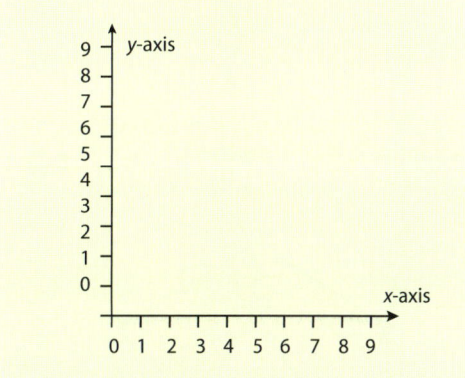

Hindu Arabic *noun*   (الأرقام) الهندية العربية
The numerals, in general use today, developed in India and Arabia

The Hindus in India had symbols for the numerals 1 to 9 over 2000 years ago.

Hindu numerals

The Arabs developed the numerals and added a symbol for 0.

Arabic numerals
0 1 2 3 4 5 6 7 8 9

Hindu -Arabic numerals

The *Hindu-Arabic* system has been in use for nearly 12 centuries.

hypotenuse *noun*   وتر المثلث القائم الزاوية
The side opposite the right angle in a right-angled triangle

In △ ABC, AC is the *hypotenuse* and the longest side.
See Pythagoras' theorem

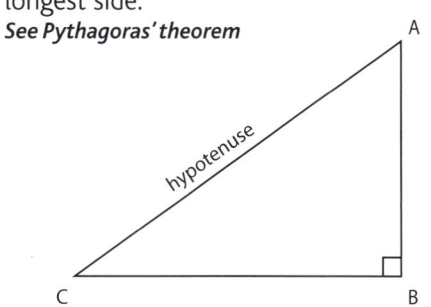

Ii

icosahedron
noun   مجسم ذو عشرين وجهًا

A regular icosahedron has 20 equilateral triangular faces, 12 vertices and 30 edges
See equilateral, -hedron, solid or 3D shapes

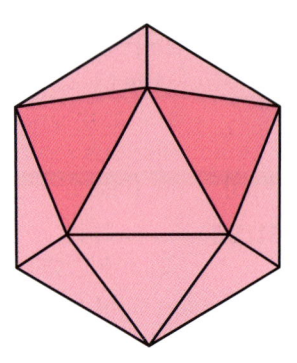

identity   *noun*   مطابقة
In algebra the equation $(a - 1)^2 = (a + 1)(a - 1)$, is known as an identity because it is satisfied by all values of 'a' it can be written using the identity sign ($\equiv$): $(a - 1)^2 \equiv (a + 1)(a - 1)$

Other equations such as $b = 4$ are satisfied by two values only; +2 and -2.
See equation

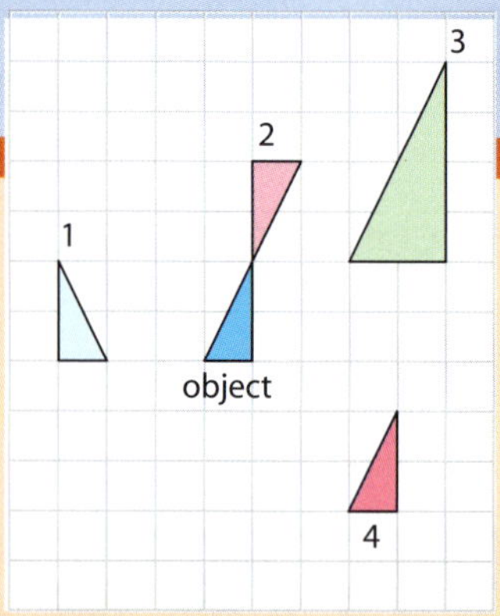

image   *noun*   صورة
When an object is moved in some way, or transformed, an image is produced
Image 1 is a reflection as in a mirror.
Image 2 is a rotation through 180°.
Image 3 is an enlargement – the base and height are doubled.
Image 4 is a translation – 3 squares to the right and 3 squares down.
See reflection, rotate translation

improper fraction
noun   كسر غير حقيقي (بسطه أكبر من مقامه)

The numerators of improper or vulgar fractions are larger than their denominators

$\frac{8}{3}$ is an example of an *improper fraction.*

An *improper fraction* can be changed into a mixed number: $\frac{8}{3} = 2\frac{2}{3}$

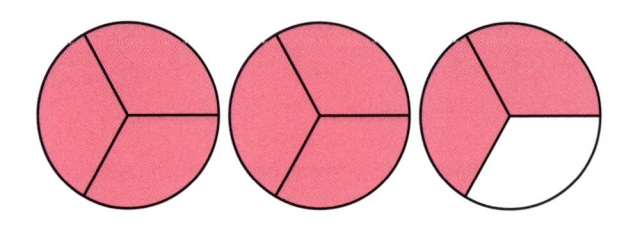

36

incentre
noun   مركز الدائرة الداخلة للمثلث

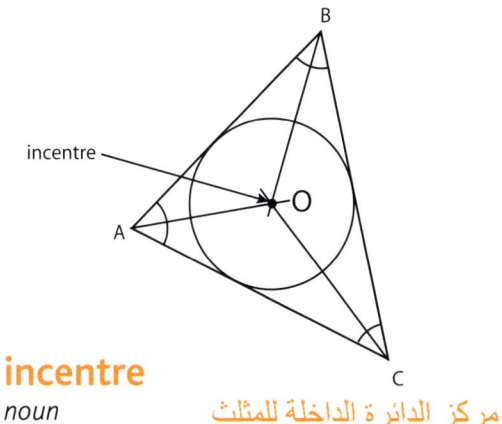

The bisectors of the internal angles of △ABC meet at O; O is the incentre of △ABC

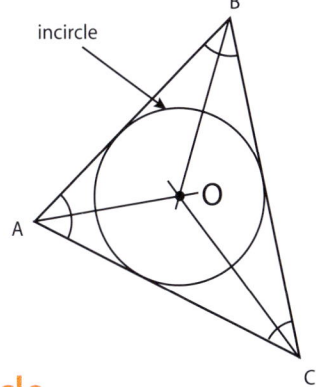

incircle
noun   الدائرة الداخلة للمثلث

A circle within a triangle which touches all the sides of a triangle

The circle, centre O, touches the sides AB, BC and CA of △ABC. AB, BC and CA are tangents to the *incircle*.

independent variable
noun   متغير مستقل

In graphing, the *x*-axis shows a range of values or the independent variable
The *y*-axis shows the corresponding range of dependent values.
In graphing the circumferences (C) of circles with a range of diameters (d), C is the dependent variable and d is the *independent variable.*
See axis

inequality

index   noun   الأس / قوة العدد
Another term for exponent or power
In 2^3, 3 is the *index*. 2^3 can be referred to as 'two cubed' or 'two to the power of three'.
$2^3 = 2 \times 2 \times 2$
In 3^2, 2 is the *index*. 3^2 can be referred to as 'three squared' or 'three to the power of two'.
$3^2 = 3 \times 3$
See exponent

indirect proportion
noun   تناسب عكسي

Indirect or inverse proportion is a relationship between two variable quantities *a* and *b*, such as $a = k\frac{1}{b}$, where *k* is a constant
See direct proportion

inequality   noun   متباينة
A relationship between two values which indicates how they compare but that they are not equal. In mathematics, inequality is represented using the signs > (greater than) and < (less than)
For example:
If a and b represent two values their *inequality* relationships may be:
$a > b$ (a is greater than b)
$a < b$ (a is less than b)
$b > a$ (b is greater than a)
$b < a$ (a is less than a)
See greater/less than

infinite

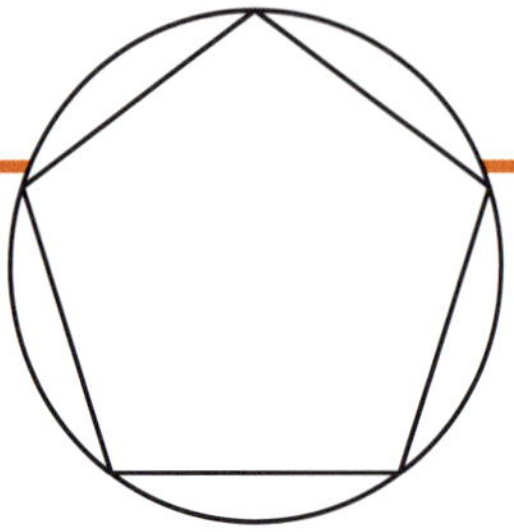

infinite *adjective* لا نهائي
Not finite – having a size or value that is greater than any number
For example, the set of counting numbers is *infinite*. If set A is the set of counting numbers then set A is written:
Set A = {1, 2, 3 ... ∞}, where ∞ is the symbol for *infinity*.

infinity *noun* لا نهاية
The idea of something that is limitless – so vast, or constantly growing, that it can never be measured
The universe stretches to *infinity*, so no matter how many millions of miles you travel or for how long, you will never reach its end.
A number that is so great that it can never be reached is known as *infinity* (∞).
See finite

inscribe *verb* يحيط بـ
The construction of a geometric figure inside another so that there are no intersections
For example, the pentagon is *inscribed* in the circle.

integer *noun* عدد صحيح
Positive or negative whole number including zero; also known as a directed number
This line shows *integers* from -5 to +5

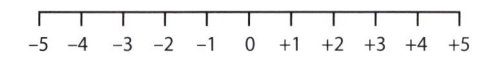

−5 −4 −3 −2 −1 0 +1 +2 +3 +4 +5

intercept *noun* الجزء المقطوع من محور الصادات
Where a line or curve crosses the *y*-axis
For the equation
$y = 2x + 3$
the *intercept* on the *y*-axis is 3.

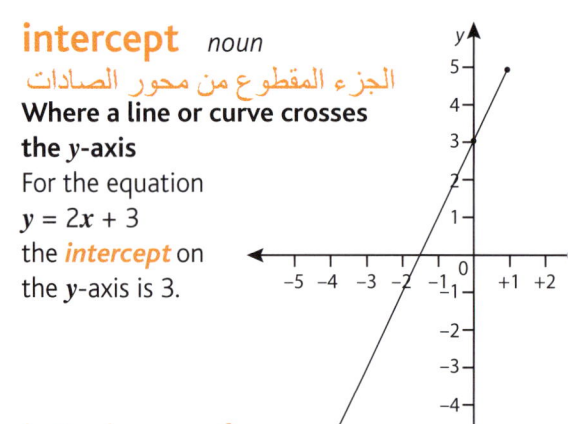

interior angle *noun* زاوية داخلة
An angle formed by adjacent sides of a polygon and lying within the figure
One of the *interior angles*, ∠ a, of the concave polygon below is a reflex angle. The *interior angles* of regular polygons are equal.
See exterior angle

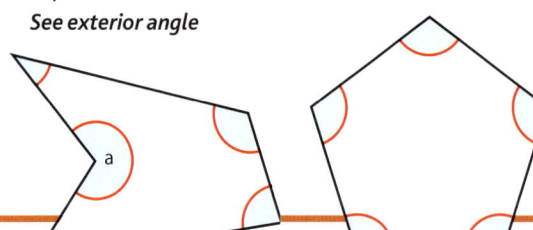

38

isosceles

International system of measurement
noun   النظام الدولي للقياس
See Système international

intersect   verb   يتقاطع
To cut across; when two straight lines intersect, four angles are formed at the point of intersection
AB and CD *intersect* at O. O is the point of *intersection*.
∠ AOD, ∠ DOB, ∠ BOC and ∠ AOC are formed at the point of *intersection*.

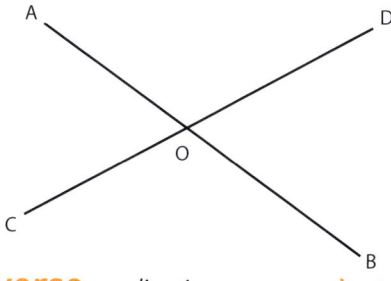

inverse   adjective   معكوس/ نظير
An inverse operation is the opposite or reverse of an earlier statement
The *inverse* of multiplication is division
5 x 4 = 20   20 ÷ 4 = 5

inverse   noun   معكوس/ نظير
The opposite of a number
When dividing by a fraction the result is the same as multiplying by its *inverse*, for example:
Division by a fraction: $2 \div \frac{1}{4} = 8$

Multiplication by its inverse: $2 \times \frac{4}{1} = 8$

inverse proportion
noun   تناسب عكسي
See indirect proportion

invert   verb   يعكس / يقلب
To turn upside down
When you *invert* the fraction $\frac{1}{4}$ you produce its inverse $\frac{4}{1}$.

irrational   noun   غير نسبي
A value which cannot be expressed as a whole number or an exact fraction
For instance, the value of pi (π).

$$\pi = \frac{\text{circumference}}{\text{radius}}$$

The value of π is defined as *irrational*. Its nearest value involving fractions is $\frac{22}{7}$ or $3\frac{1}{7}$. Most often the value of π is given as 3.142 to three decimal places. π is now known to over 2000 million decimal places but a final value will never be known.
See circle, pi (π)

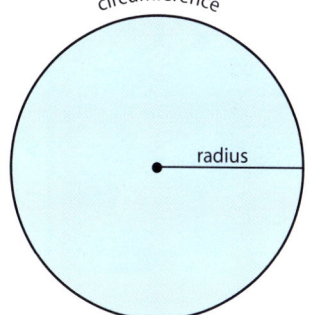

isosceles   adjective   متساوي الساقين
Type of triangle having two equal sides
The base angles opposite the equal sides are also equal.
See triangle

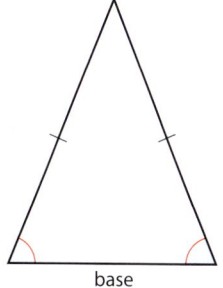

39

Kk

kilo-
prefix   كيلو: بادئة بمعنى ألف
Metric system prefix for 1000
See kilogram, kilometre, kilolitre, metric and SI units

kilogram *noun*   كيلو جرام
Symbol: kg; 1000 grams = 1 kg;
1000 g = 1 kg
Where small objects are usually weighed in grams, larger objects, such as people, are weighed in *kilograms*.
See metric and SI units

kilolitre *noun*   كيلولتر
Symbol: kl
1000 litres = 1 kl; 1000 l = 1 kl
See metric and SI units

kilometre *noun*   كيلو متر
A measurement of distance in which 1 kilometre (km) is equal to 1000 metres (m)
Layla cycles 2 *kilometres* to school each day.
See metric and SI units

kite *noun*   طائرة ورقية
A plane or 2D shape which has two pairs of equal adjacent sides; its diagonals intersect at right angles

knot
noun   عقدة: ميل بحري في الساعة
The speed of ships or boats and aircraft is given in knots (kn); kt and kts are other symbols used for knot
1 kn = 1 nautical mile per hour
1 kn = 1.85 km/h
The *knot* is not an International System of Measurement unit.
See Système International

Ll

(LCD) Lowest common denominator
noun   المقام المشترك الأصغر

The lowest common multiple of the denominators of a group of fractions

For example, 2, 3 and 6 are the denominators of these fractions:

$$\frac{1}{2} \quad \frac{2}{3} \quad \frac{5}{6}$$

The *lowest common denominator* of 2, 3 and 6 is the lowest number that they will divide into exactly. The common denominator of 2, 3 and 6 is one of the common multiples of 2, 3 and 6. These are 6, 12, 18, 24 ...
The lowest (or least) common multiple (LCM) is 6 and becomes the *LCD* for the fractions.

$$\frac{1}{2} \quad \frac{2}{3} \quad \frac{5}{6} \text{ can be written with an } \textit{LCD} \text{ of 6 } \quad \frac{3}{6} \quad \frac{4}{6} \quad \frac{6}{6}$$

The *LCD* is used when adding or subtracting fractions.
See *LCM*

(LCM) Lowest common multiple
noun   المضاعف المشترك الأصغر

The lowest number which each member of a group of numbers will divide into

For example:
The LCM of 2, 6 and 9

Multiples of 2
2, 4, 6, 8, 10 12, 14, 16, 18 20, 22, 24, 26 28, 30, 32, 34, 36 ...

Multiples of 6
6, 12, 18, 24, 30, 36 ...

Multiples of 9
9, 18, 27, 36, 45 ...

The common multiples of 2, 6 and 9 are 18, 36 ...
The least, or *lowest common multiple* is 18.

length   *noun*   طول
The distance between A and B is the length of the line segment AB or |AB|

A •————————————————————• B

Length is one of the dimensions of a 2D and a 3D figure.

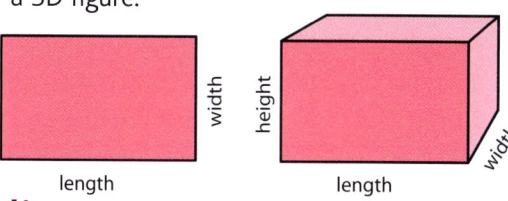

line   *noun*   خط
A one-dimensional figure of no thickness; it may be curved or straight

The shortest distance between two points is always a straight *line*.

line graph

line graph
noun   التمثيل بالخط البياني
A type of graph that uses one or more lines to display information
See graphs

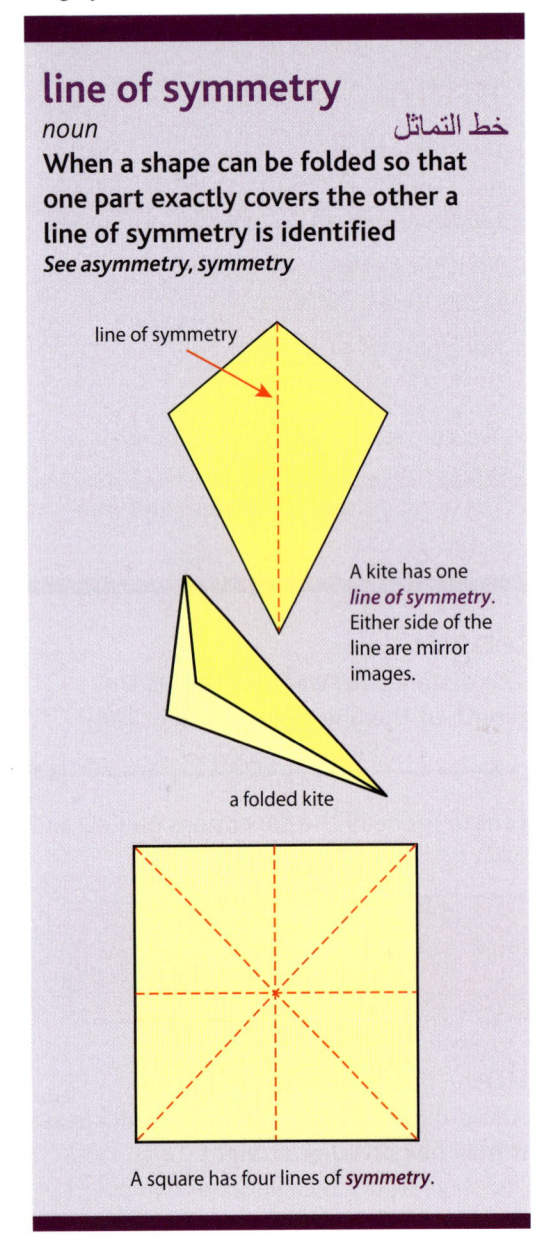

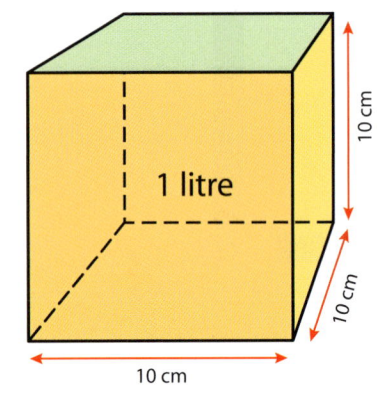

line of symmetry
noun   خط التماثل
When a shape can be folded so that one part exactly covers the other a line of symmetry is identified
See asymmetry, symmetry

line of symmetry

A kite has one *line of symmetry*. Either side of the line are mirror images.

a folded kite

A square has four lines of *symmetry*.

10 cm · 10 cm · 10 cm · 1 litre

litre   noun   لتر
Metric unit of capacity used most often to measure liquids (l)
1 *litre* (l) of water weighs 1 kilogram (kg) and has a volume of 1000 cubic centimetres (cm^3).
See metric and SI units

locus   noun   محل هندسي
A locus (plural loci) is the path followed by a point according to a rule
For example: the *locus* of points equidistant from two given points is the perpendicular bisector of the line joining the two points.

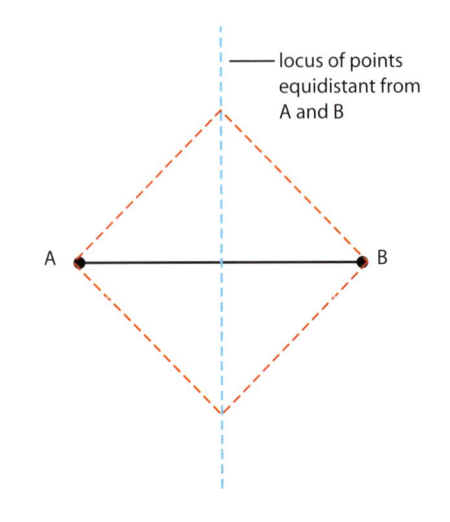

locus of points equidistant from A and B

A   B

lowest terms

logarithm noun لوغاريتم

The logarithm, to the base 10, of a number is the power to which 10 must be raised to give that number

For example:
$100 = 10^2$ The *logarithm* of 100 is 2.
$\log 100 = 2$

$1000 = 10^3$ The *logarithm* of 1000 is 3.
$\log 1000 = 3$

The *logarithm* of 532 will be between 2 and 3. It will be 2._ _ _ _. 2 is called the characteristic. The decimal part, called the mantissa, is taken from *logarithm* tables.

	0	1	2	3	4	5	6	7	8	9
53	7243	7251	7259	7267	7275	7284	7292	7300	7308	7316

$\log 532 = 2.7259$ because $532 = 10^{2.7259}$

long division noun القسمة المُطوَّلة

An algorithm for division by a divisor with more than 1 digit that proceeds by identifying multiples for the quotient and subtracting from the dividend and partial dividends

```
              28.7        Quotient
   Divisor  17)489.3      Dividend
              34
              ---
              149
              136      Partial dividends
              ---
              133
              119
              ---
              14
```

long multiplication noun الضرب المُطوَّل

An algorithm for multiplication by a multiplier with more than 1 digit that proceeds by identifying partial products and adding them to attain a final product

```
   347        Multiplicand
 x  26        Multiplier
 ----
  2082        6 x 347 Partial product
  6940        10 x 2 x 347
 ----
  9022        product
```

lowest terms noun أبسط صورة

The expression of a fraction in the lowest possible numbers

A fraction is reduced to its *lowest terms* by dividing its numerator and denominator by common factors.

$15 \div 3 = 5$

$$\frac{15}{24} = \frac{5}{8}$$

$24 \div 3 = 8$

3 is a common factor of 15 and 24.
See common factor, denominator, numerator

43

Mm

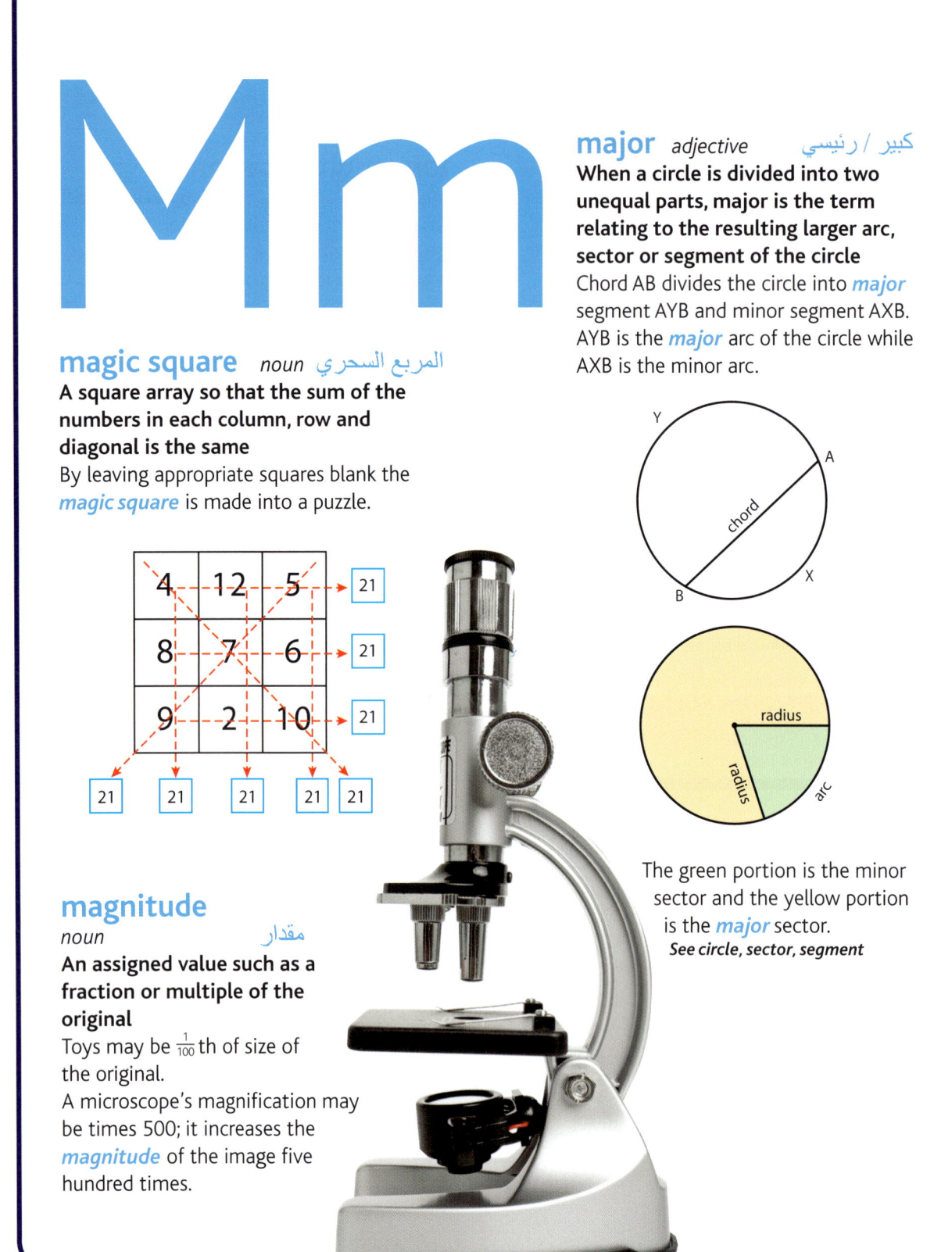

magic square noun المربع السحري

A square array so that the sum of the numbers in each column, row and diagonal is the same

By leaving appropriate squares blank the *magic square* is made into a puzzle.

4	12	5	→ 21
8	7	6	→ 21
9	2	10	→ 21

21 21 21 21 21

magnitude
noun مقدار

An assigned value such as a fraction or multiple of the original

Toys may be $\frac{1}{100}$ th of size of the original.

A microscope's magnification may be times 500; it increases the *magnitude* of the image five hundred times.

major adjective كبير / رئيسي

When a circle is divided into two unequal parts, major is the term relating to the resulting larger arc, sector or segment of the circle

Chord AB divides the circle into *major* segment AYB and minor segment AXB. AYB is the *major* arc of the circle while AXB is the minor arc.

The green portion is the minor sector and the yellow portion is the *major* sector.

See circle, sector, segment

maximum

mantissa
noun   الجزء العشري في اللوغاريتم

The fraction part of a logarithm
See logarithm

mass   *noun*   كتلة

The amount of matter something contains

The *mass* of an astronaut on the Moon and on the Earth is the same but their weight is different due to gravity.
Mass is measured using the metric units gram, kilogram and tonne.
See metric and SI units, weight

matching
verb   توفيق / مقابلة

A process, using one-to-one correspondence, by which it can be determined that one set is equivalent, larger or smaller than another

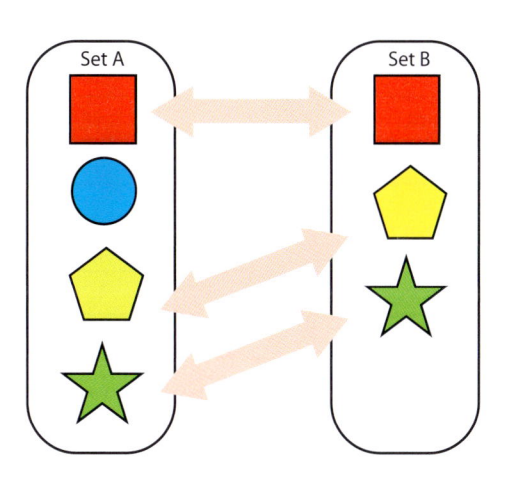

Set A   Set B

Set A > Set B   Set B < Set A

mathematics   *noun*   الرياضيات

At primary and secondary school, some pure and applied mathematics topics are studied; pure mathematics includes arithmetic, geometry, algebra, coordinate geometry, trigonometry and calculus
When you go to your *mathematics* lessons, you will study a combination of these different *mathematical* subjects.
Applied *mathematics* includes statistics and mechanics.

matrix   *noun*   مصفوفة

An array of numbers such as:

$$\begin{pmatrix} 1 & 3 \\ 4 & 2 \end{pmatrix} \text{ or } \begin{pmatrix} 1 & 0 & 1 \\ 0 & 1 & 1 \end{pmatrix}$$

See array

maximum   *adjective*   العظمى

The highest value of a set of values

For example, in a range of values 1–100, 100 is the *maximum* value.
Rashid's father wanted to take all his four children and his wife to the cinema, but he found that the *maximum* number of tickets that he could get was five, so he realised that his wife and children could go, but he would have to stay at home.

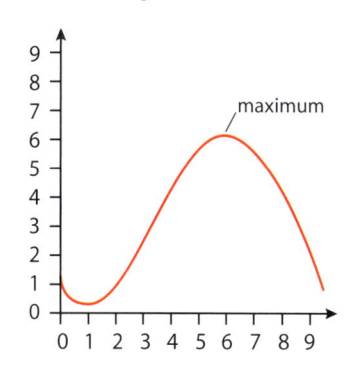

45

mean

mean noun   الوسط الحسابي
A measure of central tendency or middleness; the arithmetic mean or average of a set of values is found by adding them and dividing by the number of values
See arithmetic mean, median, mode

median noun   الوسيط
In statistics, a measure of central tendency; the median of a set of values is found by arranging them in ascending or descending order and identifying the middle value
For an even number of values the mean of the middle two values is taken as the *median*.
See mean, mode

median noun   الخط المنصف
In geometry, a median is a straight line, from a vertex of a triangle, to the midpoint of the opposite side
See centroid, midpoint

mega- prefix   ميجا
Prefix for a multiple of a million or 10^6 in some units of the metric system
See metric and SI units

member noun   عضو / عنصر
Another name for element of a set
Just as brothers and sisters are *members* of the set 'family', so 2 and 4 are *members* of the set 'even numbers'.
See set

metre noun   متر
Metric unit of length
The definition of the *metre* (m) was originally one ten-millionth of the distance from the equator to the North Pole. The *metre* is divided into 100 centimetres (cm) and 1000 millimetres (mm). 1000 m = 1 kilometre (km).
An athletics running track is 400 *metres* around, and the straight is 100 *metres* long.

metric and SI units
noun   النظام المتري ووحدات القياس الدولية
Metric prefixes

Prefix	Abbreviation	Factor
tera-	T	10^{12}
giga-	G	10^{9}
mega-	M	10^{6}
kilo-	k	10^{3}
hecto-	h	10^{2}
deca-	da	10^{1}
deci-	d	10^{-1}
centi-	c	10^{-2}
micro-	µ	10^{-6}
nano-	n	10^{-9}
pico-	p	10^{-12}
femto-	f	10^{-15}
atto-	a	10^{-18}

metric and SI units

Length   الطول
10 mm = 1 cm
10 cm = 1 dm
10 dm = 1 m (metre)
10 m = 1 dam
10 dam = 1 hm
10 hm = 1 km

Most common usage
1000 mm = 1 m
100 cm = 1 m
1000 m = 1 km
See length

Area   المساحة
100 mm² = 1 cm²
100 cm² = 1 m² (square metre)
100 m² = 1 are (a)
100 are (a) = 1 hectare (ha)
100 ha = 1 km²

Other connections
10 000 cm² = 1 m²
10 000 m² = 1 hectare (ha)
1 000 000 m² = 1 km²
See area

Volume   الحجم
1000 cm³ = 1 dm³
1 000 000 000 dm³ = 1 km³
See Système international, volume

Mass   الكتلة
10 mg = 1 cg
10 cg = 1 dg
10 dg = 1 g (gram)
10 g = 1 dag
10 dag = 1 hg
10 hg = 1 kg
1000 kg = 1 tonne

Most common usage
1000 mg = 1 g
1000 g = 1 kg
1000 kg = 1 tonne (t)
See mass

Capacity   السعة
10 ml = 1 cl
10 cl = 1 dl
10 dl = 1 l (litre)
10 l = 1 dal
10 dal = 1 hl
10 hl = 1 kl

Most common usage
1000 ml = 1 l
1000 l = 1 kl
See capacity

midpoint

midpoint noun نقطة المنتصف
A point exactly halfway between two points on a straight line
In geometry, a straight line from a vertex of a triangle to the *midpoint* of the opposite side is called a median.

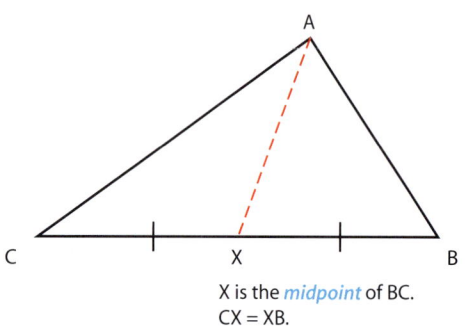

X is the *midpoint* of BC.
CX = XB.
See median

milliard noun مليار
Old name for a thousand million (no longer used) – now known as a billion – 10^9
See billion

minimum noun الصغرى
The opposite of maximum; the least value of a set of values
In a range of values 1–100, 1 is the *minimum* value.
See maximum

minor adjective الأصغر
When a circle is divided into two unequal parts, minor is the term relating to the resulting smaller arc, sector or segment of the circle; the opposite of the term major
See major

minuend noun المطروح منه
The number, from which, values are subtracted
For example: in the subtraction: 17 - 9 = 8
17 is the *minuend*
A number which is subtracted is called a subtrahend and the result is called the difference.
Here the subtrahend is 9 and the difference is 8.
See difference, subtraction, subtrahend

minus sign noun علامة الطرح (ناقص)
Minus (-) is the name of the sign for subtraction
See signs, subtraction

mixed adjective مختلط / متنوع
Not of the same type or 'varied'
In fractions, a *mixed* number has a whole number part and a fractional part.
$2\frac{1}{2}$ is a *mixed* number.

mode noun المنوال
In statistics, a measure of central tendency; the mode of a set of values is the most frequent value, the one that occurs most often
In the set of values 4,4,5,6,8,9, the *mode* is 4 because it is the value which occurs most frequently.
See mean, median

multiplier

multiple noun مضاعف
Any number which is a product of a stated number and a multiplier
The *multiples* of 5 are:

5 x 1 5 x 2 5 x 3 5 x 4 5 x 5 ....
= 5   = 10   = 15   = 20   = 25

The *multiples* of 5 are also divisible by 5.
The *multiples* of 5 are listed in the 'table of fives'.
See multiplication

multiplicand noun المضروب
Any number which is multiplied or acted upon by a multiplier to form a product
For example:

6 x 1 6 x 2 6 x 3 6 x 4 6 x 5 ...
= 6   = 12   = 18   = 24   = 30

Here 6 is the *multiplicand* and 1, 2, 3, 4, 5 are the multipliers of 6, 12, 18, 24, 30 are the products.
See multiplier, multiplication, product

multiplication noun عملية الضرب
The process by which the product is identified
For example:

multiplier
6 x 8 = 48 ← product
↑
multiplicand

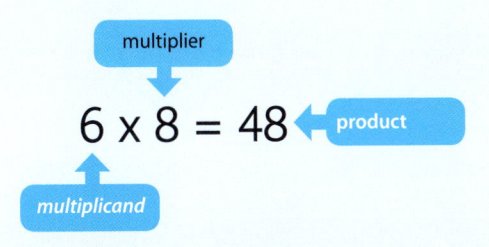

See multiplicand, multiplier, multiplication, product, signs

multiplication grid جدول الضرب
A listing in table form of the products from the top row and the first column of a group of numbers
In the table below, the products along the diagonal of the grid are square numbers.

×	0	1	2	3	4	5	6	7	8	9	10	11	12
0	0	0	0	0	0	0	0	0	0	0	0	0	0
1	0	1	2	3	4	5	6	7	8	9	10	11	12
2	0	2	4	6	8	10	12	14	16	18	20	22	24
3	0	3	6	9	12	15	18	21	24	27	30	33	36
4	0	4	8	12	16	20	24	28	32	36	40	44	48
5	0	5	10	15	20	25	30	35	40	45	50	55	60
6	0	6	12	18	24	30	36	42	48	54	60	66	72
7	0	7	14	21	28	35	42	49	56	63	70	77	84
8	0	8	16	24	32	40	48	56	64	72	80	88	96
9	0	9	18	27	36	45	54	63	72	81	90	99	108
10	0	10	20	30	40	50	60	70	80	90	100	110	120
11	0	11	22	33	44	55	66	77	88	99	110	121	132
12	0	12	24	36	48	60	72	84	96	108	120	132	144

multiplier noun المضروب فيه
In multiplication, the value that acts on the multiplicand to form the product
For example, in this calculation:

17 x 3 = 51
3 is the *multiplier*.

See multiplicand, multiplication, product

Nn

nano-
prefix نانو: بادئة بمعنى جزء من ألف مليون

Used in front of units to multiply that unit by 10 to the power of -9, making it a very small number; $10^{-9} = 0.000\ 000\ 001$

A *nanosecond* is one thousand millionth of a second or 0.000 000 001 seconds.
A *nanometre* is one thousand millionth of a metre or 0.000 000 001 metres.

natural number   *noun*   عدد طبيعي

A positive integer; natural numbers are sometimes called the counting numbers
The *natural numbers* are 1, 2, 3, 4, 5, 6 ... and so on.
See integer, number

negative number   *noun*   عدد سالب

A real number that is less than zero is a negative number; a negative sign is put in front of these numbers to show they are negative

-4, -3.65, -0.01 and -$\frac{1}{4}$ are examples of *negative numbers*.

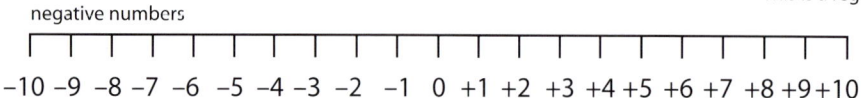

negative numbers

–10 –9 –8 –7 –6 –5 –4 –3 –2 –1 0 +1 +2 +3 +4 +5 +6 +7 +8 +9 +10

See real number, positive number

net   *noun*
شبكة المجسّم الهندسي / الأشكال المكونة للمجسّم

A flat surface made from polygons that you can fold up along the edges to make into a polyhedron
The *net* of a pyramid has a square in the middle with a triangle on each side.

Net of an pyramid

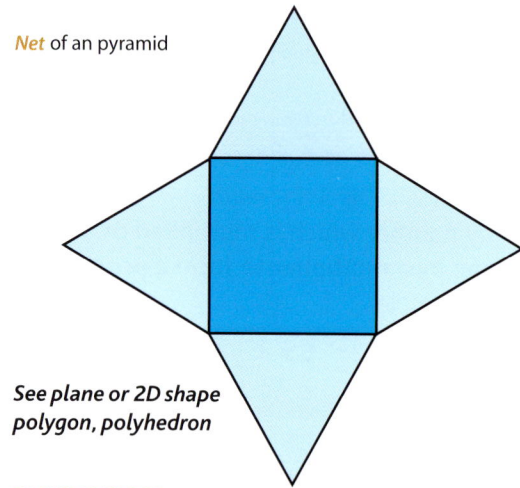

See plane or 2D shape
polygon, polyhedron

nonagon
noun   متسّع / شكل تساعي الأضلاع

A flat shape with nine straight sides

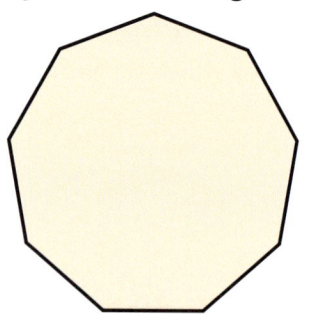

This is a regular *nonagon*.

50

number line

normal *adjective* عمودي على / متعامد على
A line is normal if it intersects another line or plane at right angles
AB is perpendicular to line CD, so AB and CD are *normal* lines.

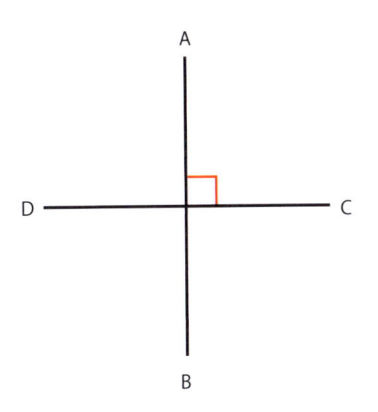

normal distribution *noun* التوزيع الطبيعي
When data is shown on a frequency diagram, there is normal distribution when the frequency diagram is symmetrical around the mean value, which is also the mode and median

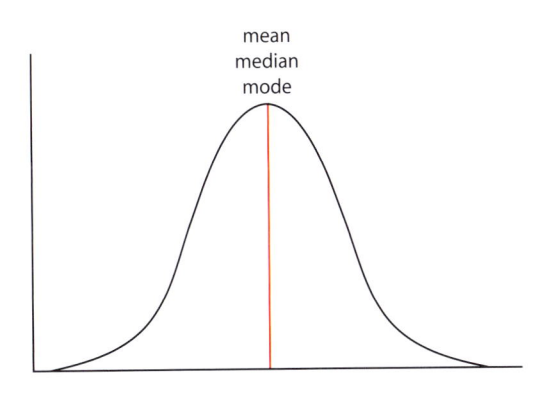

When *normal distribution* is shown like this, it is sometimes called a bell-curve.
See mean, median and mode

null set *adjective* المجموعة الخالية
If shapes, numbers or objects are sorted and there is a set which is empty, this is said to be a null set
The set of all odd numbers that are divisible by 6 is a *null set*.

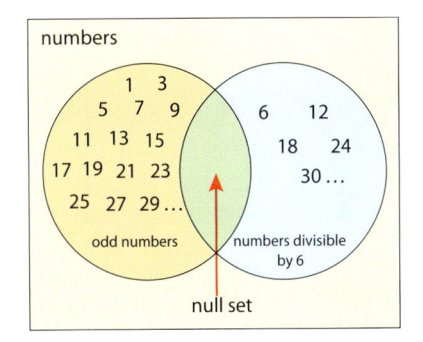

See empty set

number *noun* عدد
A symbol that is used for counting or representing an amount
When we talk about numbers we are usually referring to natural *numbers*.
Using the word 'whole' and 'negative' in front of the word 'number' shows the type of number you are describing.
13, 28 and 355 are examples of whole *numbers*.
-8, -15 and -1.7 are examples of negative *numbers*.
See natural number, negative number

number line *noun* خط الأعداد
A line with a scale showing numbers in order
A *number line* can be labelled with numbers or it can be partly numbered.
See scale

51

numeral

numeral noun
عدد

A figure written as a symbol to represent a number; numerals are made up of the digits 0, 1, 2, 3, 4, 5, 6, 7, 8 and 9

The *numeral* 5067 is five thousand and sixty-seven, and is made from the digits 5, 0, 6 and 7.

See digit

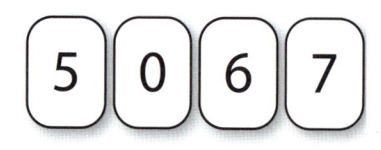

5 0 6 7

numerator noun
بسط

The number above the line in a fraction; the number below the line is the denominator and shows the number of equal parts of the fraction; the numerator shows how many of these equal parts are being used

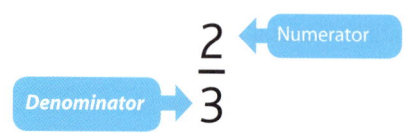

$$\frac{2}{3}$$

Numerator → 2
Denominator → 3

$\frac{2}{3}$ of 15 = 10

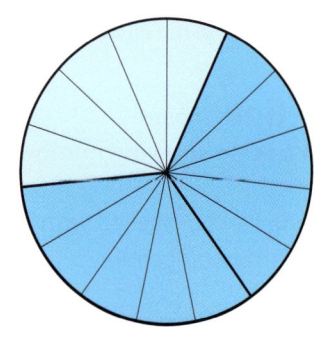

(15 ÷ 3) × 2 = 10

See denominator, fraction

numerical adjective
عددي

Relating to a number or numbers

These numbers are arranged in *numerical* order:

36   38   41   57   60

A ruler, used for measurement, is a good example of the usefulness of *numerical* order.

Oo

oblique *adjective* مائل
An oblique line is one that is slanted or sloped
This diagonal from one vertex of the rectangle to the opposite vertex is an *oblique* line.

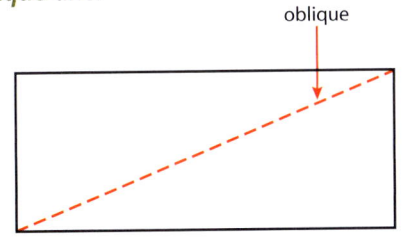

See vertex

oblong *noun* مستطيل
A rectangle with one pair of sides longer than the other pair
Oblongs and squares are both types of rectangles. A square is a special rectangle with four sides of equal length, so it is not an *oblong*.

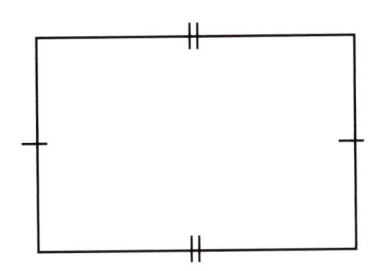

obtuse angle
noun زاوية منفرجة
An angle greater than a right angle (90°) but less than a straight line (180°)

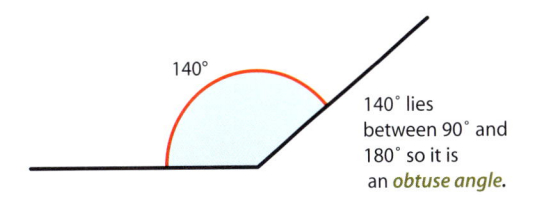

140° lies between 90° and 180° so it is an *obtuse angle*.

octagon
noun مُثَمَّن / شكل ثماني الأضلاع والزوايا
A polygon with 8 straight sides

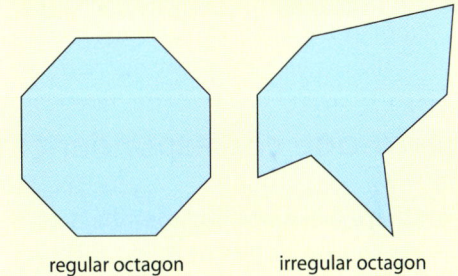

regular octagon　　irregular octagon

octahedron
noun مجسّم ثماني الأوجه
A solid shape or polyhedron, with 8 flat faces; a regular octahedron is made from 8 equilateral triangles

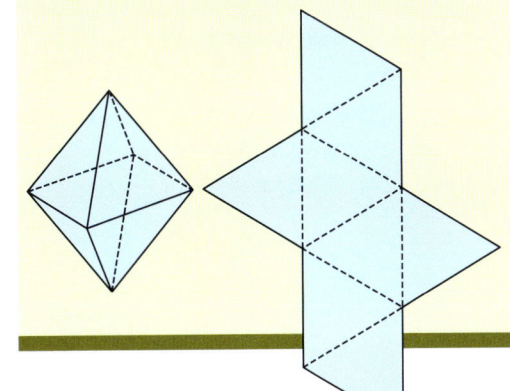

53

odd number

odd number noun   عدد فردي
When a whole number is divided by 2 and leaves a remainder of 1, it is an odd number
Odd numbers always end in the digits 1, 3, 5, 7 or 9, so the number 30225 is an *odd number* (see the blocks, below).

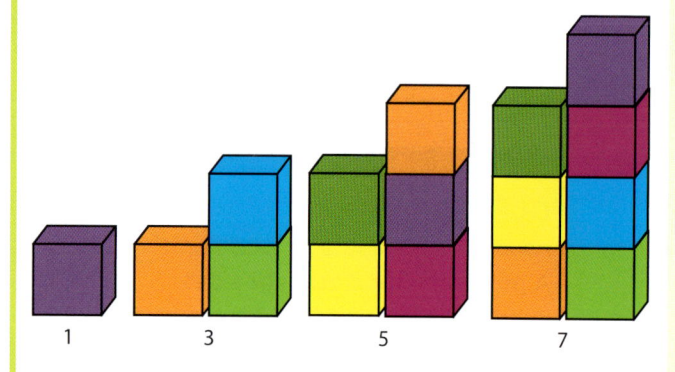

1   3   5   7

one-to-one correspondence noun   التقابل الأحادي
When there are matching members of two sets to make pairs of items, without using items in either set twice, there is one-to-one correspondence

×4
1 → 4
2 → 8
3 → 12
4 → 16

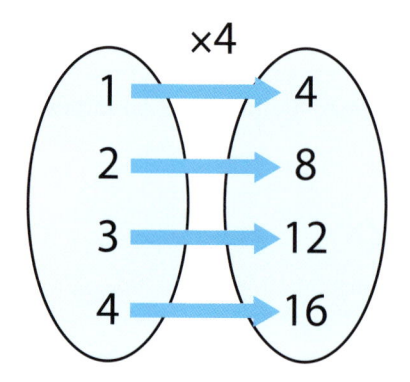

operand noun   معامل
The quantity or number on which an operation is carried out
12 x 3 = 36
12 is the *operand*. It is multiplied by 3 (the operation) to give the answer 36.

operation noun   عملية
A rule or method for changing numbers in a calculation is an operation; the four basic number operations are addition, subtraction, multiplication and division
48 − 15 = 33
The *operation* in this calculation is subtract (−).

operator noun   رمز العملية
A symbol used to show which operation is to be carried out
32 + 25 = 57
The operation is addition and the *operator* is the addition symbol (+).

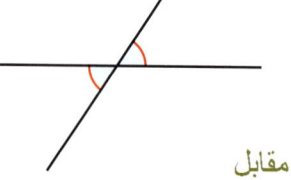

opposite
adjective   مقابل
To be in a position opposite something is to be facing it
When two straight lines cross each other, four angles are made. The angles *opposite* each other, just touching at the crossing point, are equal in size.
Opposite angles are equal in size.

order of operations

ordered pair noun   زوج مُرَتَّب
The set of two numbers written to show a position on a grid of coordinates; the *x*-number is written first, followed by the *y*-number
See coordinates

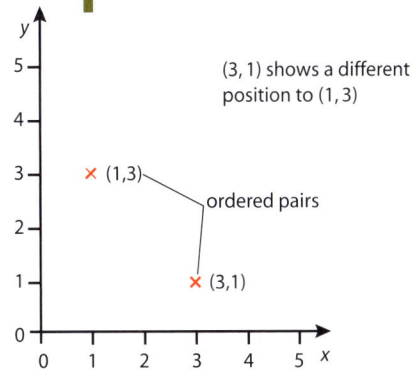

(3, 1) shows a different position to (1, 3)

ordered pairs

order of operations
noun   ترتيب العمليات الحسابية

Rules which indicate how to calculate when there are a number of operations – addition, subtraction, multiplication, division and brackets involved

The content of brackets must be calculated first. For example

5 + (4 + 3)	7 - (6 - 2)	9 + 2(8 - 5)
= 5 + (7)	= 7 - (4)	= 9 + 2(3)
= 5 + 7	= 7 - 4	= 9 + 6
= 12	= 3	= 15

When there are sets of brackets work from inside to the outside.

9 + [20 - 3(2 x 3)]
= 9 + [20 - 3(6)]
= 9 + [20 - 18]
= 9 + [2]
= 11

The *order of operations* is: Brackets Of Divide Multiply Add Subtract or BODMAS for easy recall.
See operation

If the word 'of' (meaning 'multiplies') appears that part must be worked after the brackets.

$\frac{3}{4}$ of 8 + 5(8 - 3) = $\frac{3}{4}$ of 8 + 5(5)

Brackets first.

= $\frac{3}{4}$ of 8 + 25

then 'of' $\frac{3}{4}$ of 8 = 6

= 6 + 25
= 31

After attending to any 'brackets' and 'of', work from left to right putting brackets around division and multiplication parts and calculating the outcome.

Working from left to right again, do additions and then subtractions.

20 - $\frac{8}{2}$ + 5 - 3 x (7 - 3)

Brackets. (7 – 3) = 4

= 20 - ($\frac{8}{2}$) + 5 - 3 x (4)
= 20 - (4) + 5 - [12]
= 20 + 5 - 4 - 12
= 25 - 16
= 9

order of symmetry

order of symmetry
noun   رتبة التماثل

The order of rotational symmetry of a shape is the number of times it can be turned to fit on itself until it returns to the original position

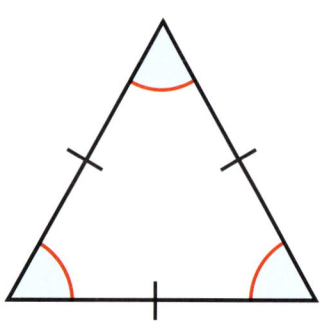

This triangle has an order of rotational symmetry of 3

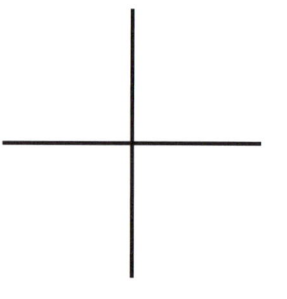

This shape has an order of rotational symmetry of 4

This snow flake has rotational symmetry of order 6

See rotational symmetry

ordinal number
noun   العدد الترتيبي

A number used to describe the position of an object in a set, when they are put in order; first (1st), second (2nd), third (3rd) and fourth (4th) are all examples of ordinal numbers

In this race, car number 32 finished just behind the winner so it was second (2nd).

See cardinal number

origin noun
نقطة الأصل

The point on a graph where the *x*-axis and *y*-axis cross, when using a coordinates system

The coordinates for the *origin* are (0,0).
See axis, coordinates

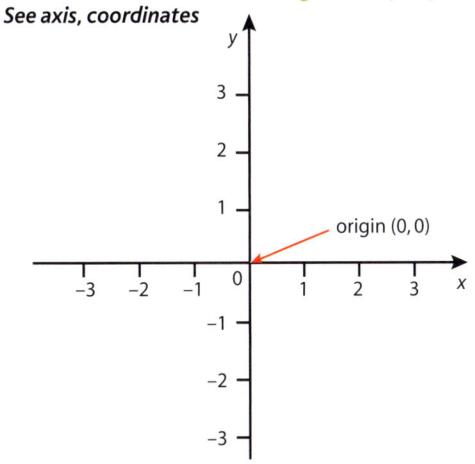

orthocentre
noun
ملتقى الارتفاعات

The point at which the three altitudes of a triangle meet
See altitudes

output noun
إنتاج / مُخرَجات

The amount produced by a machine or process is the output; it is the opposite of input

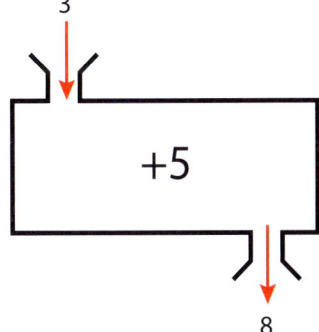

In this instance, the input is 3 and the *output* is 8.

oval

oval noun
بيضاوي

A flat egg-shaped object or an ellipse

Even though many dinner plates are round, many serving plates are *oval*.

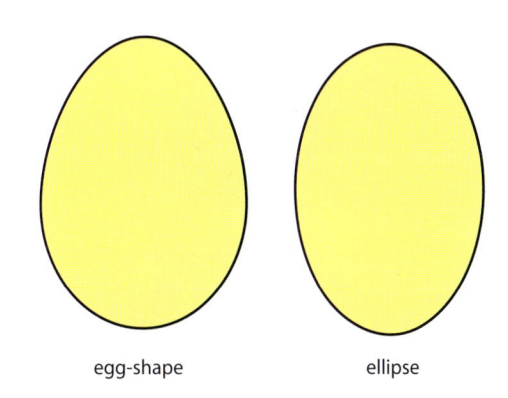

egg-shape   ellipse

57

P p

pair noun
زوج

A set of two objects
A trapezium has a *pair* of parallel sides.
There are three *pairs* of shoes.

parallel adjective
مُوازي / مُتوازي

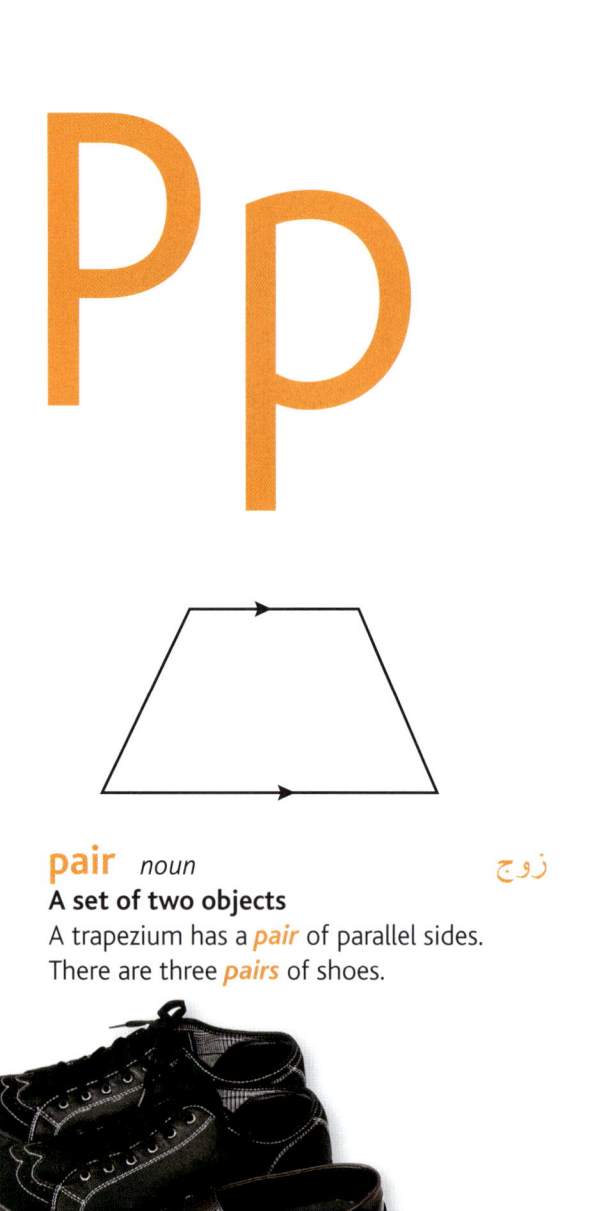

Lines that are parallel always stay the same distance apart and never meet

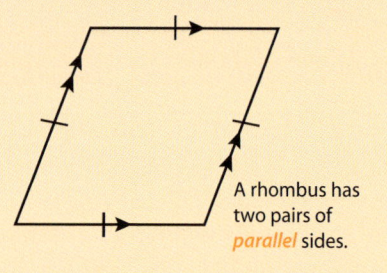

A rhombus has two pairs of *parallel* sides.

A line crossing two *parallel* lines forms corresponding angles and alternate angles.

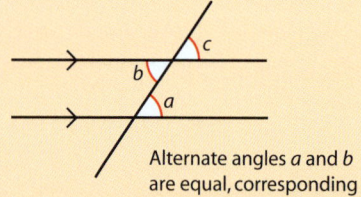

Alternate angles *a* and *b* are equal, corresponding angles *a* and *c* are equal.

parallelogram noun
متوازي الأضلاع

A quadrilateral with two pairs of parallel sides and opposite sides equal in length
The diagonals of a *parallelogram* bisect each other.

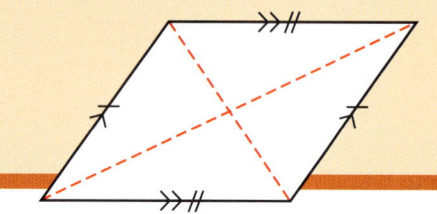

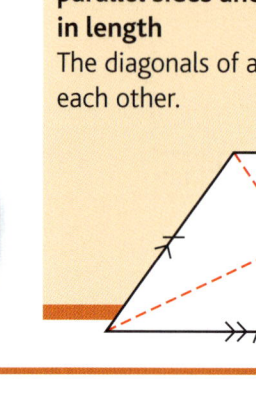

58

pentahedron

partial product
noun   حاصل الضرب الجزئي

Parts of long multiplication calculated before reaching the final answer
See long multiplication

Pascal's triangle
noun   مثلث باسكال

Numbers arranged in the shape of a triangle, with a 1 at the top and also at the two ends of each line; the other numbers are made by adding together the pair of numbers above each one

This arrangement of numbers is named after the French mathematician Blaise Pascal (1623–1662). There are many patterns and sequences within *Pascal's triangle*.

```
              1
            1   1
          1   2   1
        1   3   3   1
      1   4   6   4   1
    1   5  10  10   5   1
  1   6  15  20  15   6   1
1   7  21  35  35  21   7   1
```

pattern *noun*   نموذج / عينة / نمط

A repeated arrangement of numbers or shapes; they repeat or change in a regular way

9 18 27 36 45 54 …

The numbers in the 9 times table have a special *pattern*.

penta- *prefix*   بنتا: بادئة بمعنى خمسة

Prefix denoting five

pentagon
noun   مُخَمَّس / شكل خماسي الأضلاع

A flat shape or polygon with 5 straight sides

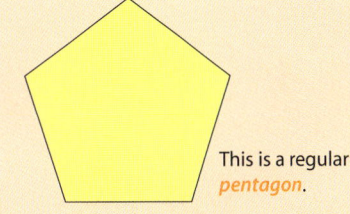

This is a regular *pentagon*.

pentahedron
noun   مجسّم خماسي الأوجه

A solid shape or polyhedron, with 5 flat faces

A square-based pyramid is a type of *pentahedron*.

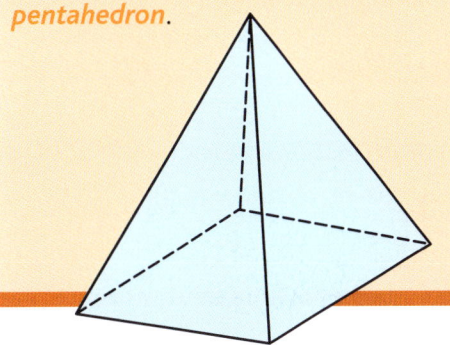

percentage

percentage noun نسبة مئوية
A fraction out of 100; it means the proportion or rate out of every 100 parts; the % sign is used to show percentages

In a class of 25 children, 15 were girls. This means that the *percentage* of girls in the class was 60%.

$$\frac{15}{25} = \frac{60}{100} \text{ is } 60\%$$

On this draughts board there are 32 black squares. This is 50% of the number of squares.

$$\frac{32}{64} = \frac{1}{2} = \frac{50}{100} \text{ is } 50\%$$

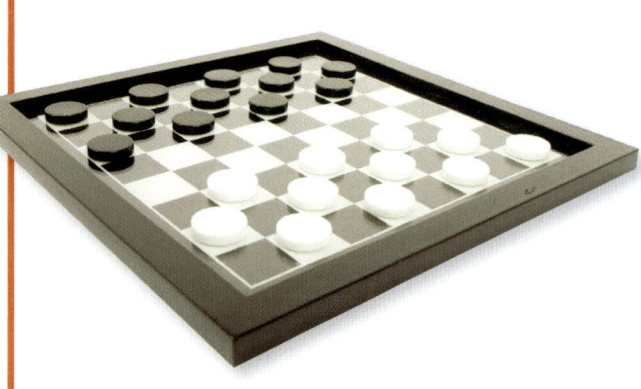

perfect number noun عدد تام
A number that is the sum of its factors (except for the number itself) is said to be a perfect number

The factors of 6 are 1, 2 and 3 (do not include 6).

1 + 2 + 3 = 6

So 6 is a *perfect number*.

The next *perfect number* is 28.

1 + 2 + 4 + 7 + 14 = 28.

See factor

perfect square noun مربع تام
A number whose square root is a whole number

16 is an example of a *perfect square* because the square root of 16 is 4.

$\sqrt{16} = 4$

$4^2 = 16$

See square root

×	0	1	2	3	4	5	6	7	8	9	10
0	0	0	0	0	0	0	0	0	0	0	0
1	0	1	2	3	4	5	6	7	8	9	10
2	0	2	4	6	8	10	12	14	16	18	20
3	0	3	6	9	12	15	18	21	24	27	30
4	0	4	8	12	16	20	24	28	32	36	40
5	0	5	10	15	20	25	30	35	40	45	50
6	0	6	12	18	24	30	36	42	48	54	60
7	0	7	14	21	28	35	42	49	56	63	70
8	0	8	16	24	32	40	48	56	64	72	80
9	0	9	18	27	36	45	54	63	72	81	90
10	0	10	20	30	40	50	60	70	80	90	100

The shaded values are the *perfect square* numbers to 100.

perimeter noun محيط
The outside edge of a shape or area, and the length of that edge

If you walk around the edge of a field, you will have walked around its *perimeter*.

See area, boundary

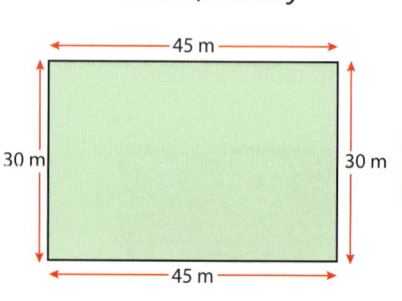

This field has a *perimeter* of 150m.

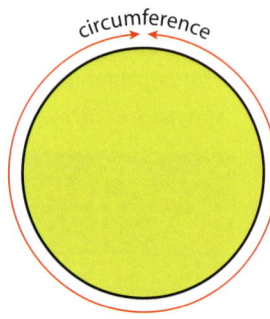

The *perimeter* of a circle is called the circumference.

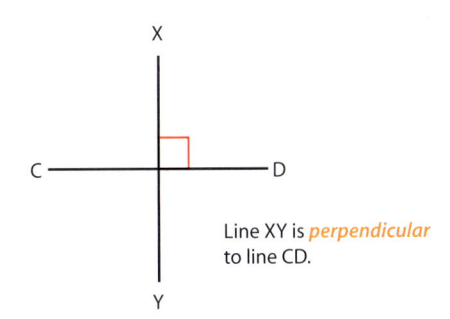

X

C —|— D

Y

Line XY is *perpendicular* to line CD.

perpendicular adjective عمودي
A line at right angles to another line
See normal

pi (π) noun النسبة التقريبية للدائرة
In a circle, pi is the ratio of its circumference to its diameter
If the circumference of a circle is divided by its diameter, the answer is always equal to *pi*, written as π. Its value is approximately 3.14, but although it is now known to over 2000 million decimal places, a final value will never be known.

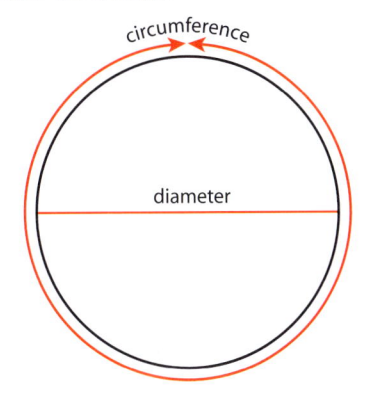

circumference

diameter

π = circumference ÷ diameter
π is approximately
3.14159265355820974944821480865 1...
See circle, circumference, diameter

pictograph noun المُصَوِّرات
A type of graph which uses pictures or symbols to show information
See graphs

place value

pie chart noun التمثيل البياني بالقطاعات الدائرية
Statistical data can be shown in a circular chart called a pie chart; the circle is divided into sectors that each represent a proportion of the whole
This *pie chart* shows the four most popular car colours sold by a dealer in a year. There were 240 cars sold altogether. The *pie chart* shows that half the cars sold were white, which is 120 white cars in total.
See graphs

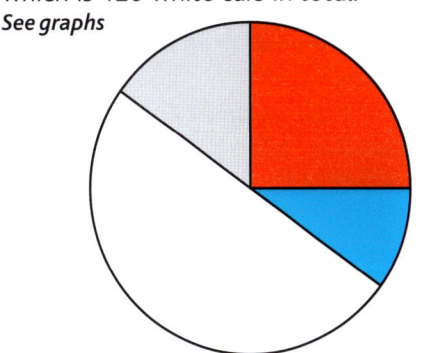

place value noun القيمة المكانية للرقم
The position or place of a digit in a number; the same digit has a different value at different positions in the number
For the number 348.25, the *place value* of the three is 300 and the 2 is $\frac{2}{10}$.
$300 + 40 + 8 + \frac{2}{10} + \frac{5}{100} = 348.25$
See digit

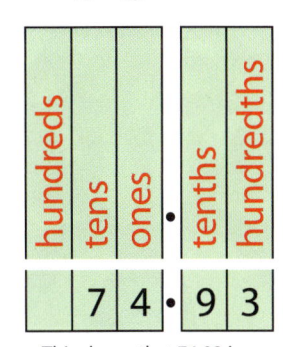

hundreds	tens	ones	.	tenths	hundredths
	7	4	.	9	3

This shows that 74.93 is
7 tens + 4 ones + 9 tenths + 3 hundredths.

plane

plane noun/adjective سطح مستوي
A flat surface; a line joining any two points lies on a flat or plane surface
The surface of a piece of paper or a table top are examples of *plane* surfaces.

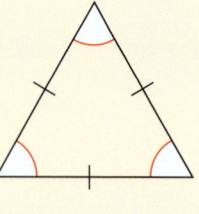

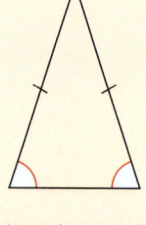

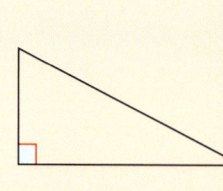

plane (or 2D) shapes
noun الأشكال ذات البعدين
Any two-dimensional (2D) or flat shape with length and width but no depth; any shape that you draw on a piece of paper would be an example of a plane figure
We are surrounded by *plane shapes* in our everyday lives, often in architectural form (for example floor and wall tiles, roof tiles).
Writing paper usually comes in the shape of a rectangle; mirrors come in a variety of shapes, for instance hexagons, circles, squares and rectangles; and stained glass windows are sometimes made up of a complex variety of regular and irregular *plane shapes*.
A flat or *2D shape* with three or more sides is known as a polygon.
See net, polygon

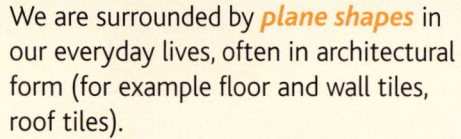

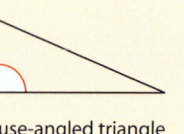

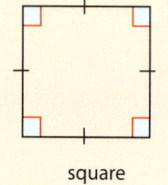

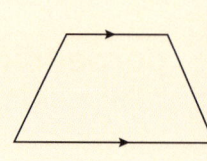

equilateral triangle

isosceles triangle

right-angled triangle

obtuse-angled triangle

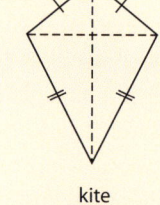

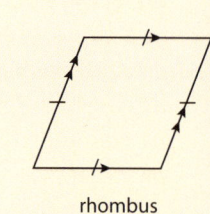

square

trapezium

parallelogram

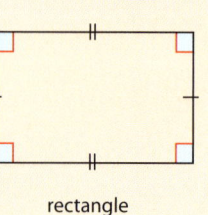

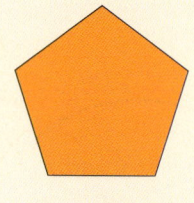

kite

rhombus

rectangle

pentagon

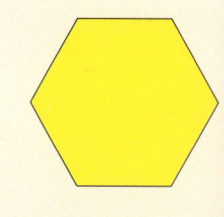

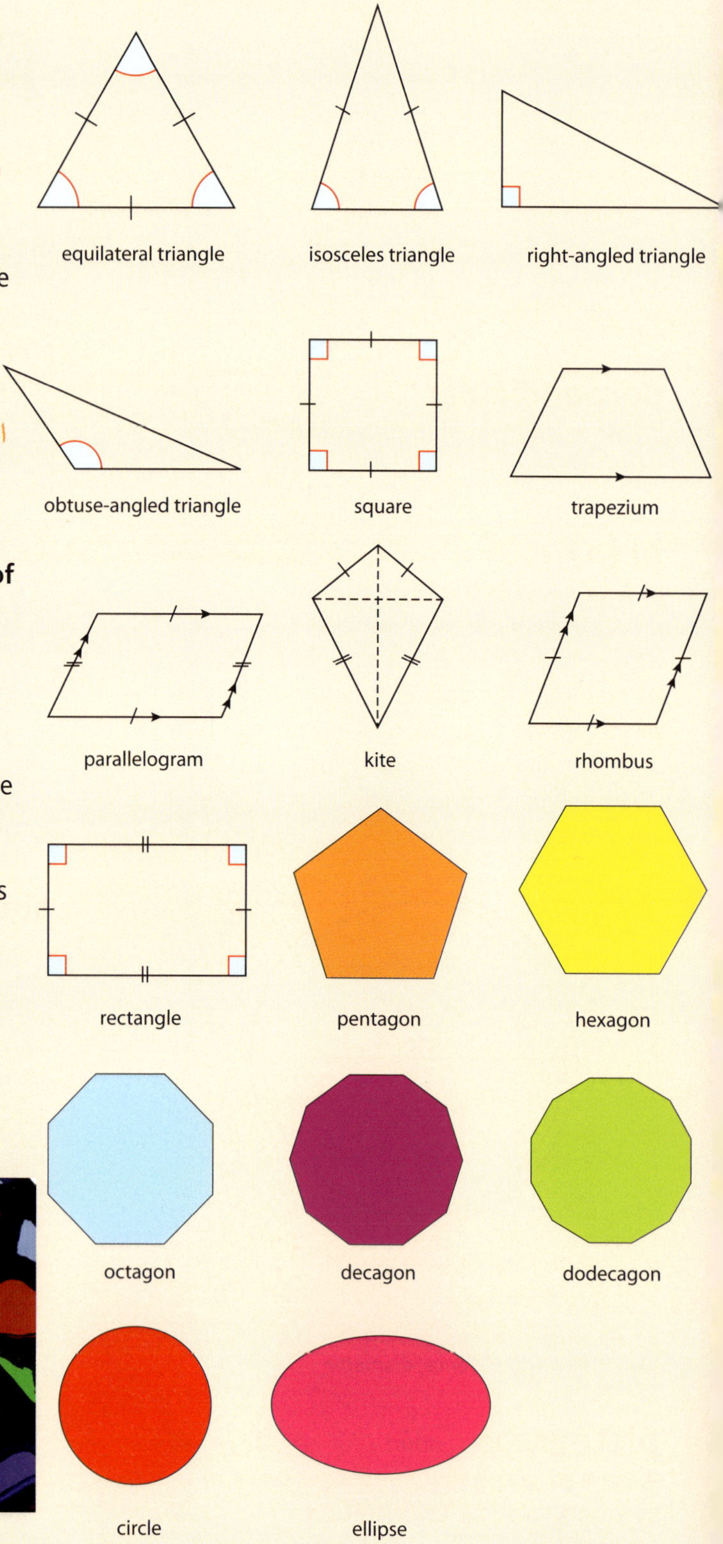

hexagon

octagon

decagon

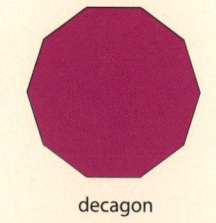

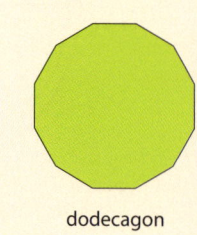

dodecagon

circle

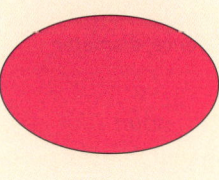

ellipse

62

polyhedron

Platonic solid *noun* متعدد السطوح
See polyhedron

plot *verb* يرسم / يخُطّ
To mark a position using coordinates you plot points on a graph
If you had collected a set of data, you could *plot* the information on a graph and then join up the points that you had *plotted* to see what the information tells you.

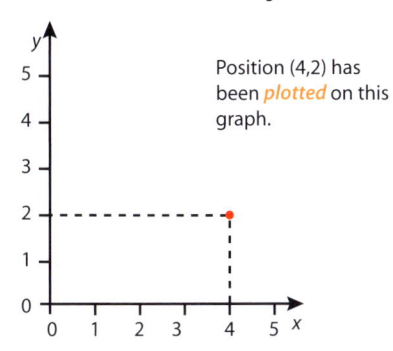

Position (4,2) has been *plotted* on this graph.

plus sign *noun* زائد
Plus means add or in addition to; the plus sign is +
6 plus 8 equals 14
6 + 8 = 14
See addition

point *noun* نقطة
A dot or mark showing a position on a graph or where lines intersect

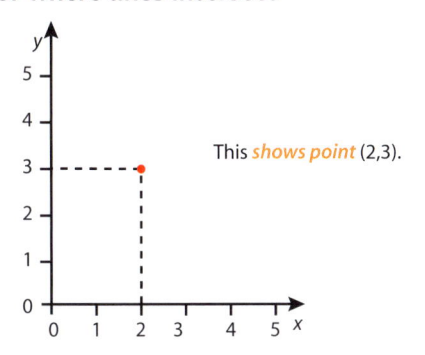

This *shows point* (2,3).

polygon *noun* مضلع
A flat or 2D shape with three or more sides
Any closed plane shape with straight sides is a *polygon*. If all the sides are equal length and all the angles are equal, then the shape is a regular *polygon*.

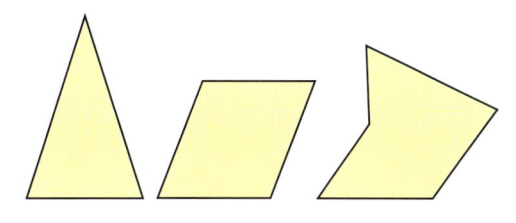

These are examples of *polygons*.

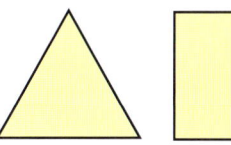

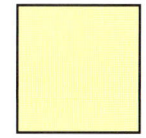

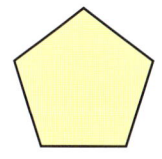

These are examples of regular *polygons*.

See regular

polyhedron *noun* متعدد السطوح
Any solid shape with faces that are polygons is a polyhedron (pl. polyhedra); also known as a Platonic solid
Here are examples of three *polyhedra*:

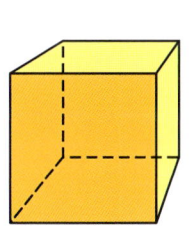

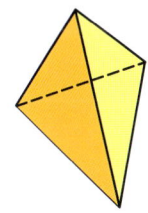

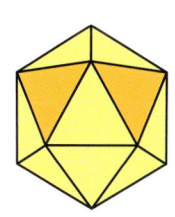

See solid or 3D shapes

63

positive number

positive number   noun   عدد موجب
Any real number that is greater than zero is a positive number
9, 30.02, 0.006 and $\frac{3}{5}$ are examples of *positive numbers*.
$x > 0$ means x is a *positive number*
See real number, negative number

power   noun   الأس / قوة العدد
See exponent, index

prime factor   noun   عامل أولي
A factor that is a prime number
The factors of 12 are 1, 2, 3, 4, 6 and 12. The *prime factors* of 12 are 2 and 3.
See factor, prime number

prime number   noun   عدد أولي
Any whole number that has only two factors, 1 and itself, is a prime number
If a whole number (apart from 1) can be divided only by itself and by 1 without leaving a remainder, then it is a *prime number*. For example, 13 can only be divided equally by 1 and 13, so it is a *prime number*.

1	2	3	4	5	6
7	8	9	10	11	12
13	14	15	16	17	18
19	20	21	22	23	24
25	26	27	28	29	30

principal   noun   مبلغ المال الأصلي
The original amount of money invested or borrowed before interest is calculated
Sam invested a *principal* sum of £300 in the bank at an interest rate of 5% per annum.

Eratosthenes, a Greek astronomer, devised the Sieve of Eratosthenes to find *prime numbers*.

Write a list of numbers in order, starting with 1. Cross out 1, leave 2 and cross out every 2nd number (4, 6, 8 etc..) Leave 3 and cross out every 3rd number (6, 9, 12 etc..) 4 is already crossed out, so leave 5 and cross out every 5th number. Continue this and when complete the numbers left uncrossed are *prime numbers*.
See factor

proper fraction

prism noun   منشور
A solid shape with the same cross-section along its length; the two end faces are matching polygons such as triangles, squares or hexagons

People sometimes hang glass *prisms* in their rooms because they catch the light and create beautiful colours.

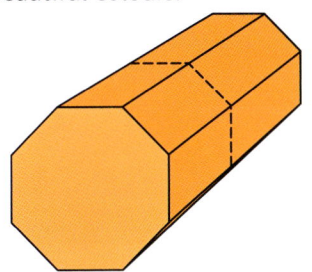

probability noun   الاحتمال
The probability of an event is a measure of the chance or likelihood that it may happen; this could be given as a fraction, a decimal or a percentage

The *probability* of rolling an even number on a dice is 1 in 2, which is $\frac{1}{2}$, 0.5 or 50%.
A *probability* scale from 0 to 1 shows the likelihood of an event happening. 0 is impossible and 1 is certain.

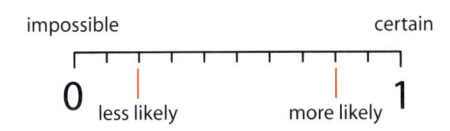

impossible   certain

0   less likely   more likely   1

product noun   حاصل / ناتج (الضرب)
When two or more numbers are multiplied together, the answer is the product of those numbers

The *product* of 3 and 5 is 15
3 × 5 = 15
3 and 5 are both factors of 15
See factor, multiplication

projection noun   إسقاط / مسقط
A mapping of points from a 3D figure onto a line or plane

An atlas is an example of a book of *projections* of different countries shown as maps.

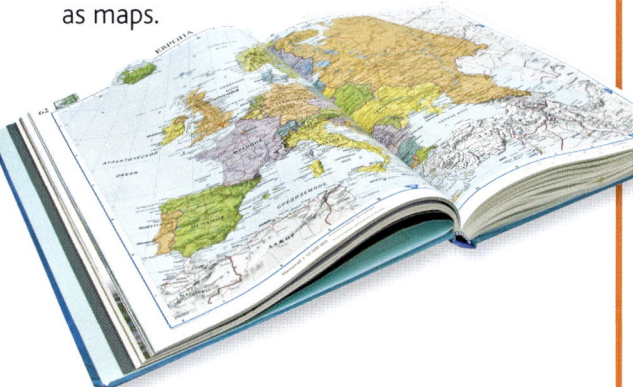

proof noun   برهان
An explanation or argument that leads to the establishment of the truth of a final statement

The *proof* for the proposition that adding two odd numbers makes an even number can be shown in this way:

Any odd number can be written as (2n + 1)

Adding two of them is

(2n + 1) + (2m + 1) = 2 (n + m) + 2 =
2(n + m + 1)

2(n + m + 1) will always be an even number.

proper fraction noun   كسر حقيقي
A fraction with a value less than 1, with the numerator smaller than the denominator

$\frac{5}{6}$ is a *proper fraction*

See denominator, improper fraction, numerator, vulgar fraction

proportion

proportion noun تناسب
Finding the proportion of an amount is the same as finding the fraction of the whole amount; a proportion can be written as a fraction
The *proportion* of the circle that is blue is 2 out of 6 or $\frac{1}{3}$.

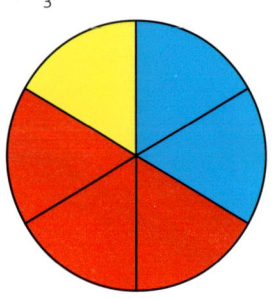

protractor noun المِنقلة
An instrument used for measuring angles. It has a scale that is marked in degrees
See angle, degrees

pure mathematics
noun الرياضيات البحتة
A branch of mathematics which studies systems and structures in the abstract, without relating to nature or practical life
See applied mathematics

square-based pyramid

pyramid noun هرم
A solid shape with triangular faces meeting at a point called a vertex
The base of a *pyramid* can be any polygon, such as a triangle, square or hexagon. This is sometimes used to name the *pyramid*.
See polyhedron, vertex

Pythagoras' theorem
noun نظرية فيثاغورث
This states that in a right-angled triangle the square on the hypotenuse is equal to the sum of the squares on the other two sides
Pythagoras was a Greek mathematician who lived in the 6th century BC. *Pythagoras'* theorem was conceived thousands of years ago, but is still used by mathematicians today.
See hypotenuse

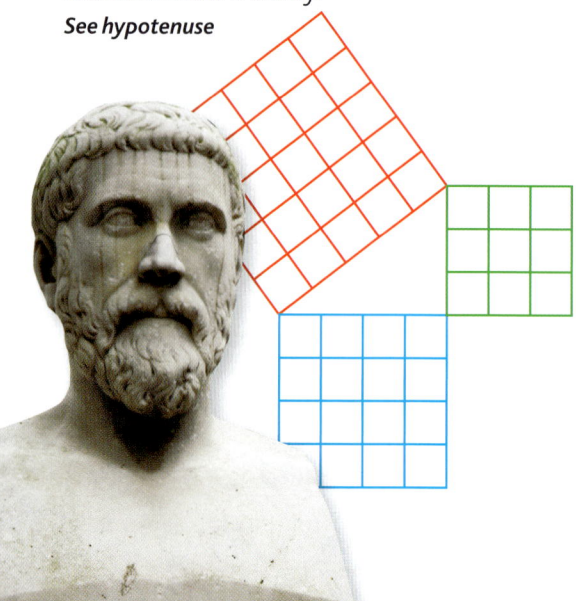

PITAGORA

66

Qq

quadrant noun   ربع الدائرة
One quarter of a circle
A quarter of a pizza is a *quadrant*.

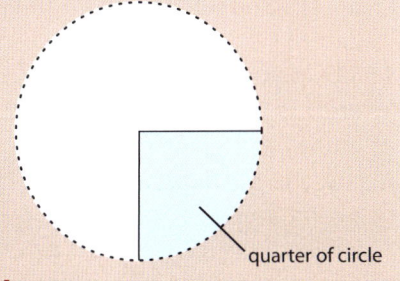

quarter of circle

quadrant noun   أحد أرباع شبكة الإحداثيات
One of the four regions on a graph or coordinates grid
A graph is divided into four *quadrants* by the *x*-axis and *y*-axis.

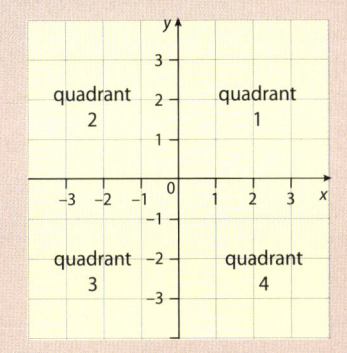

quadrant 2 | quadrant 1
quadrant 3 | quadrant 4

quadrilateral noun   رباعي الأضلاع
Any polygon with 4 sides is a quadrilateral
These are all examples of *quadrilaterals*.
See polygon

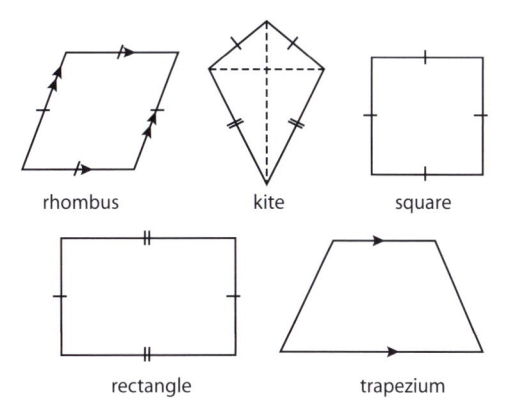

rhombus   kite   square
rectangle   trapezium

quarter noun   ربع
A quarter is one of four equal parts; one-quarter $\frac{1}{4}$, is one-fourth part of a whole
In order to share a pomegranate equally between four people it would need to be cut into *quarters*.

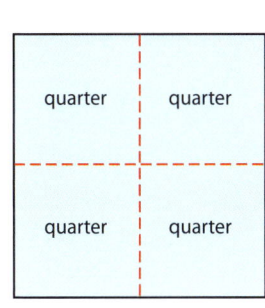

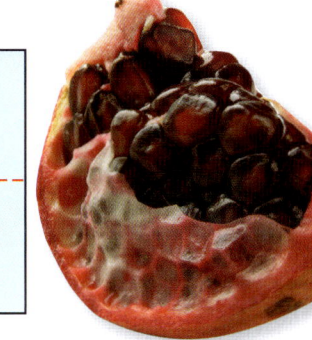

quarter | quarter
quarter | quarter

quotient noun   خارج القسمة
The result of dividing one number by another
When you divide 35 by 5, the *quotient* is 7.
See division

67

Rr

radius noun نصف القطر
The length of a straight line from the centre of a circle to its circumference
For example, if someone talks about an area within a *radius* of four kilometres of your school – they have drawn an imaginary circle around the school, with the school in the centre, and the circle four kilometres from the school in every direction. The area they are talking about is everywhere inside that circle.

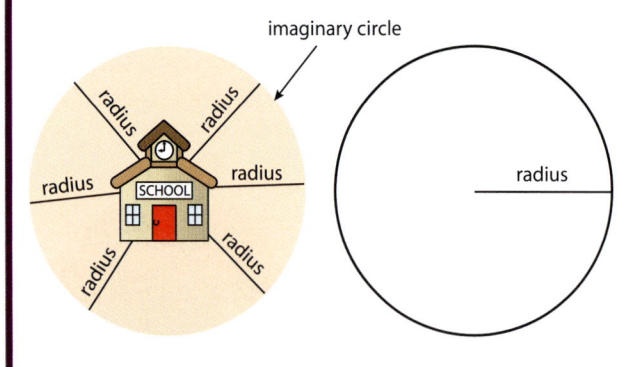

See circle

random adjective عشوائي
Something that happens purely by chance or without bias
The numbers in a lottery are drawn out at *random* so that there is an equal chance of each number being chosen.

range noun المدى
The difference between the greatest and least values in a set of data; the range is the spread of that data
The scores in a test out of 100 *ranged* from 48 to 83. The *range* of scores is 35.
See data

rate noun معدل
The ratio of one quantity to a unit of another is the rate
Speed is the *rate* of distance covered in a certain time, for example the number of kilometres travelled per hour (km/h).

rate noun معدل / نسبة
Interest is charged on an amount of money at a given rate
A bank charged a *rate* of 5% on a loan to a company.

ratio noun نسبة
Ratio compares one part or amount with another. It gives a part-to-part comparison
The *ratio* of yellow to red squares is 6 to 9 or 2 to 3. For every 2 yellow squares there are 3 red squares. This can be written as 2:3. If this pattern continued with the same *ratio* of 2:3 until there were a total of 50 squares, there would be 20 yellow squares and 30 red squares.

68

reduce

rational numbers
noun   الأعداد النسبية

Numbers that can be written in the form of $\frac{x}{y}$ where *x* and *y* are both integers and *y* is not zero

$7, 2\frac{1}{4}, 4.9, 0.08, -3$ are all examples of *rational numbers* as they can be written as

$\frac{7}{1}$ $\frac{9}{4}$ $\frac{49}{10}$ $\frac{8}{100}$ and $-\frac{3}{1}$

See integers, irrational numbers

real number   *noun*   عدد حقيقي

The set of real numbers is made up of all the rational and irrational numbers

See integer, irrational numbers, rational numbers

reciprocal   *noun*   مقلوب / معكوس

The inverse of any number apart from zero; the reciprocal of a number is the value of it when 1 is divided by that number

The *reciprocal* of 7 is $1 \div 7$ which is $\frac{1}{7}$.

See inverse

rectangle   *noun*   مستطيل

A quadrilateral with two pairs of opposite sides that are equal and parallel; each angle is 90° and the diagonals bisect each other

Many sports, for instance football and tennis, are played on *rectangular* pitches or courts.

See plane or 2D shapes, quadrilateral

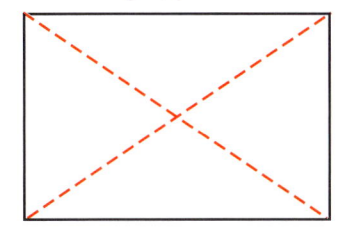

rectangular number
noun   عدد مستطيل (عوامله تشكل مستطيل)

A number that can be shown as an arrangement of squares or dots in the shape of a rectangle

Rectangular numbers must have at least two factors bigger than 1, so they are not prime numbers.

Ten is an example of a *rectangular number* (factors are 2 and 5).

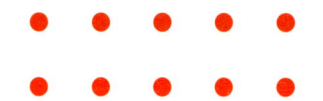

recurring decimal
adjective   كسر عشري دوري

A decimal fraction that goes on repeating itself in a continuous pattern without end

Examples:

0.3333333 ... can be written as $0.\dot{3}$ to show that the 3 recurs.

0.2525252 ... (written as $0.\dot{2}\dot{5}$).

Recurring decimals are rational numbers.

reduce   *verb*   يختزل / يختصر

To make smaller in size

This grid has been *reduced* by a scale factor of $\frac{1}{2}$.

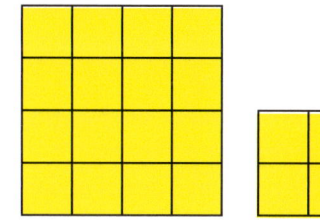

A fraction can be *reduced* by cancelling it to its lowest terms.

$\frac{12}{16}$ *reduced* to its lowest terms is $\frac{3}{4}$

reflection

reflection noun انعكاس
An image seen in a mirror; a shape with a mirror image so that both images look the same has line or reflection symmetry
Each time you look in the mirror you see your *reflection*.
See image

reflex angle noun زاوية منعكسة
An angle greater than a straight line (180°), that lies between 180° and 360°
See acute angle, obtuse angle

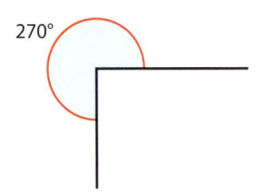

270°

regular adjective منتظم
Regular means equal or unchanging
These are all *regular* polygons.
A *regular* polygon has sides of equal length and angles of equal size.

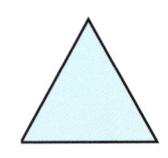

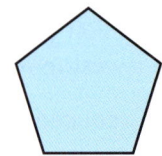

remainder noun باقي
When a number cannot be divided exactly by another number, there is a whole number answer with a remainder or an amount left over
32 ÷ 5 = 6 remainder 2

rhombus noun معين / الشكل المعين
A quadrilateral which is a special parallelogram, with 4 equal sides and no right angles
The diagonals bisect each other at right angles and are also the lines of symmetry of the *rhombus*.
See bisect

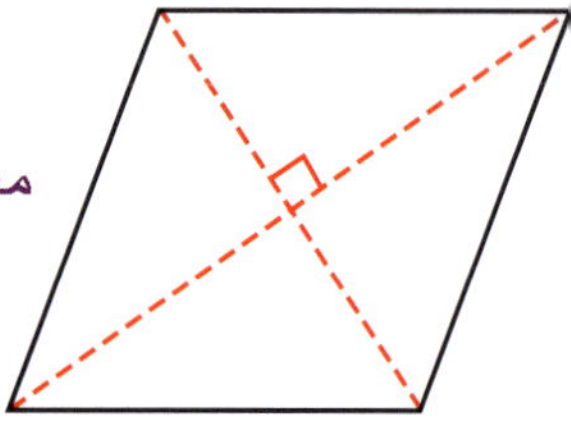

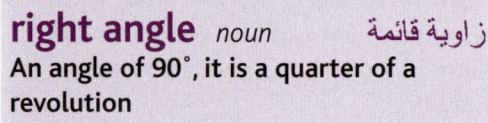

right angle noun زاوية قائمة
An angle of 90°, it is a quarter of a revolution
In a square or rectangular room, the walls meet at *right angles*.

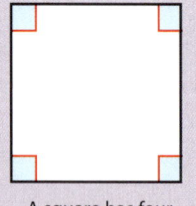

A square has four *right angles*.

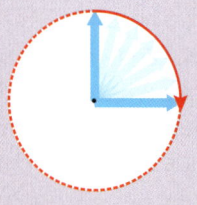

This shows 90° as a quarter of a full revolution.

right-angled triangle noun مثلث قائم الزاوية
A triangle with one of the angles at 90°
Pythagoras' theorem refers only to *right-angled triangles*.

row

Roman numerals
noun الأعداد الرومانية

These were the numerals used by the ancient Romans as part of their number system

Roman numerals used different letters for ones, tens, hundreds and thousands, but had no symbol for zero.

III	IV	V	X	L	C	M
3	4	5	10	50	100	1000

rotate verb يدور
To turn around

When a shape is *rotated* it is turned around a centre of rotation, clockwise or anticlockwise.
See anticlockwise, clockwise

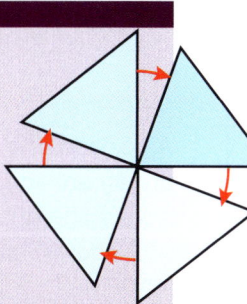

rotational symmetry
noun تماثل دوراني

A shape has rotational symmetry if there are a number of different positions the shape can take and still fit into itself, when rotated around a point

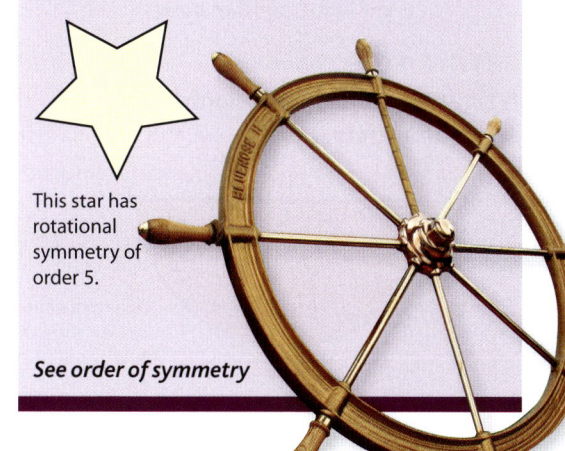

This star has rotational symmetry of order 5.

See order of symmetry

round
adjective/verb دائري
Shaped like a circle

round
verb يُقرِّب
To round a number up or down is to express it to a required degree of accuracy

When dealing with whole numbers, these can be *rounded* up or down to the nearest 10, 100 or 1000 to make them easier to work with. Decimal numbers can be *rounded* to the nearest whole number or tenth.
3435 is 3440 *rounded* to the nearest 10 and 3400 *rounded* to the nearest 100.
7.846 is 7.8 to the nearest tenth and 8 to the nearest whole number.
Where the original number ends in 5, 50, 500 etc the usual practice is to *round* up.

This CD is *round*.

row noun صف
A horizontal arrangement of objects or numbers

The middle *row* of numbers is 15, 16, 17 and 18.

11	12	13	14
15	16	17	18
19	20	21	22

See column

Ss

scale noun   مقياس الرسم

Scales show the relationship between distances on paper and real distances on the ground

Maps and drawings of buildings have *scales*.

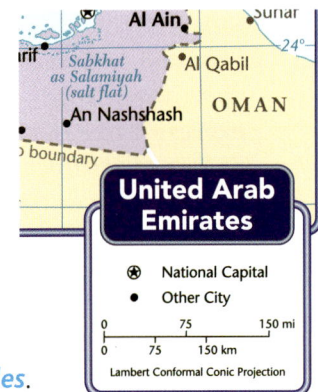

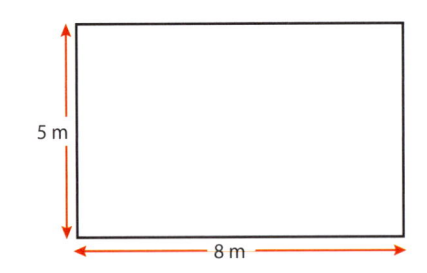

This classroom's real length is 8 m and its width is 5m.

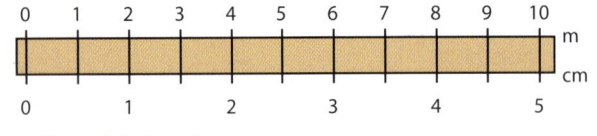

The *scale* is: 1 cm: 2 m.

scalene noun   مختلف الاضلاع

A scalene triangle has all sides unequal and hence all angles unequal

AB ≠ BC ≠ AC

See triangle

sector noun   قطاع دائري

A portion of a circle whose boundaries are two radii and an arc

See circle

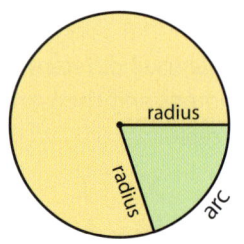

In this diagram, the green portion is the minor *sector* and the yellow portion is the major *sector*.

segment noun   قطعة دائرية

A portion of a circle whose boundaries are an arc and a chord

AB is a chord.
AXB and AYB are arcs.

See circle

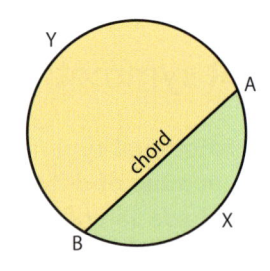

The portion AYB is the major *segment* and AXB is the minor *segment*.

semicircle noun   نصف دائرة

A figure bounded by a diameter and an arc; half a circle

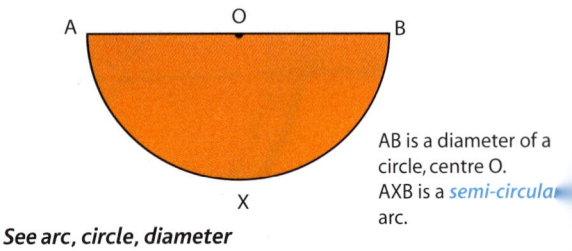

AB is a diameter of a circle, centre O.
AXB is a *semi-circular* arc.

See arc, circle, diameter

72

significant figures

sequence *noun* متتالية
The order that something happens or exists in
The *sequence* of whole numbers is 0, 1, 2, 3 ... The *sequence* of counting numbers is 1, 2, 3 ... Each number in a *sequence* is called a term.
See term

series *noun* متسلسلة
A set of numbers which are connected by a definite law
Each number in a *series* is called a term.
See arithmetic progression, geometric progression

set *noun* مجموعة
A collection of things; a set can be defined by listing its elements or members
For example, {1, 2, 3, ...} is a set of all positive integers. {a, e, i, o, u} is a set of vowels.
A family is an example of a *set* of people.

set-square *noun* مثلث للرسم الهندسي
A piece of mathematical drawing equipment in the shape of a right-angled triangle used for drawing accurate right angles; one or more of the edges may be marked up as a ruler

sexagesimal *adjective* نظام القياس الستيني (وحدته الرقم ستون)
Relating to or based on systems of measurement to a base of 60
Time is a *sexagesimal* system in which 60 seconds make 1 minute and 60 minutes make 1 hour.
See base

short division *noun* قسمة مختصرة
An algorithm for division by a small divisor that proceeds by identifying multiples for the quotient and subtracting mentally from sections of the dividend

divisor 6)5 2⁴3¹8 dividend
              8 7 3   quotient

$52 \div 6 = 8$ (nearest multiple)
Write 8 under the 2
$6 \times 8 = 48$. $52 - 48 = 4$. Write 4 next to the 3.
$43 \div 6 = 7$ (nearest multiple)
Write 7 under the 3
$6 \times 7 = 42$. $43 - 42 = 1$. Write 1 next to the 8.
$18 \div 6 = 3$. Write 3 under the 8.

significant figures *noun* أرقام معنوية
Significant figures (s.f.) in a number are counted from the first non-zero digit
$0.03264 = 0.0326$ (3 s.f.) The first, second and third *significant figures* in 0.03264 are 3, 2 and 6.

signs

signs noun   إشارات / رموز

Symbols which either act as an instruction to tell us what we should do with the numbers given to us, or else something about that number

+

plus   جمع / زائد

The addition, add or *plus* sign tells us that the numbers we have should be added together to calculate the total. For example, if you have a bag with 9 oranges in and your friend adds another 4 oranges, you will have a total of 13 oranges.

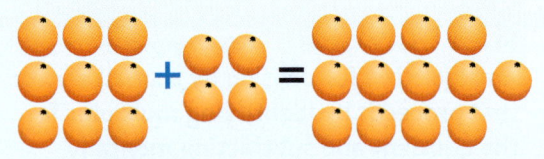

In arithmetic this would be written:
9 + 4 = 13

If you are adding larger numbers, you would set the sum out differently, in columns, to make the calculation easier to see, for example:

```
  Th H T U
     5 3 6 7    ← addends
  + 2 8 3 6
     8 2 0 3    ← total/sum
```

If the + sign is put directly in front of a number, it can also be used to indicate that the number is a positive number, that is, greater than 0.

minus   طرح / ناقص

The *minus*, subtract or take away sign tells us that we should take one number away from another to calculate the difference. For instance, if you have 17 sweets in a bag, and your friends take away 9 of them, you will have 8 sweets left.

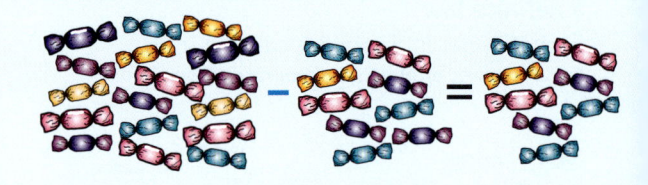

In arithmetic, this would be written:
17 − 9 = 8

If you are subtracting larger numbers, you would set the sum out in columns to make the calculation easier to see, for example:

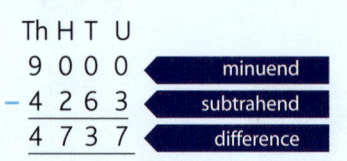

```
  Th H T U
     9 0 0 0    ← minuend
  − 4 2 6 3    ← subtrahend
     4 7 3 7    ← difference
```

If the − sign is put directly in front of a number, it can also be used to indicate that the number is a negative number, that is, less than 0.

74

signs

✕ multiply   ضرب

The multiplication or times sign tells us that we need to *multiply* a particular number a certain number of times to calculate the product. For instance, if seven students enter the classroom, each carrying six books, all together they will be carrying 42 books.

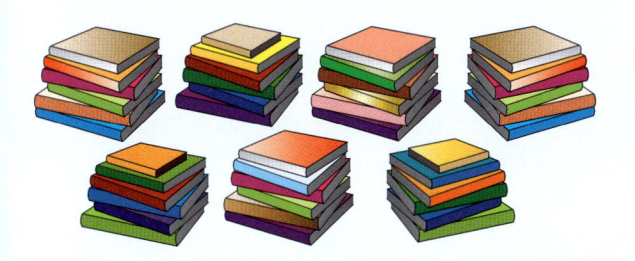

In arithmetic this would be written:
7 x 6 = 42

For larger numbers, the sum would be set out in columns to make the calculation easier to see. For example:

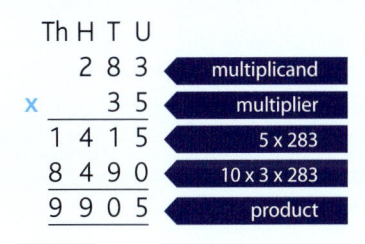

```
    Th H T U
         2 8 3    ← multiplicand
    x      3 5    ← multiplier
    ─────────
       1 4 1 5    ← 5 x 283
       8 4 9 0    ← 10 x 3 x 283
    ─────────
       9 9 0 5    ← product
```

÷ divide   قسمة

The division or *divide* by sign tells us that we need to split, or *divide* a particular number into a certain number of smaller amounts to calculate the quotient. For example, if the teacher asked a class of 24 children to *divide* into groups of three, there would be eight groups of children.

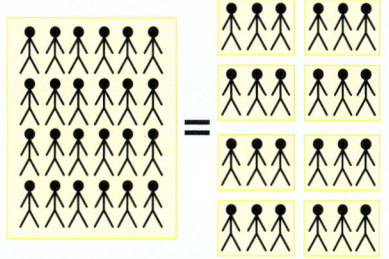

In arithmetic this is written: 24 ÷ 3 = 8
For larger numbers, the calculation would be set out differently. Either

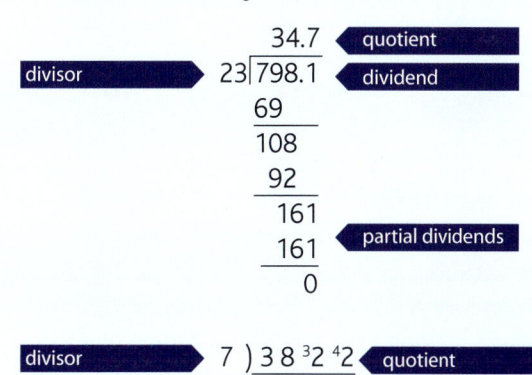

```
                      34.7         ← quotient
    divisor →    23 ) 798.1        ← dividend
                      69
                      ───
                      108
                       92
                      ───
                      161          ← partial dividends
                      161
                      ───
                        0
```

```
    divisor →   7 ) 3 8 ³2 ⁴2      ← quotient
                    5 4 6          ← dividend
```

38 ÷ 7 = 5 (nearest multiple) write 5 under the 8
7 x 5 =35, 38 -35 = 3 write 3 next to the 2
32 ÷ 7 = 4 (nearest multiple) write 4 under the 2
7 x 4 = 28, 32 -28 =4 write 4 next to the 2
42 ÷ 7 =6 write 6 under the 2

signs

=

equals   يساوي

The *equals* sign means that whatever quantity is on one side of the sign is the same as whatever quantity is on the other. For example, if Marie holds five cherries, Ahmed holds four and Walid holds eight, while Yasmin holds a box containing seventeen cherries, Marie, Ahmed and Walid together hold the same number of cherries as Yasmin.

In arithmetic this would be written:
5 + 4 + 8 = 17

≠

not equal to   لا يساوي

This sign represents not *equal to*, and is the opposite to =.
If Marie were holding eight cherries, with Ahmed holding four and Walid holding eight, together they would no longer be holding the same number of cherries as Yasmin.
8 + 4 + 8 ≠ 17

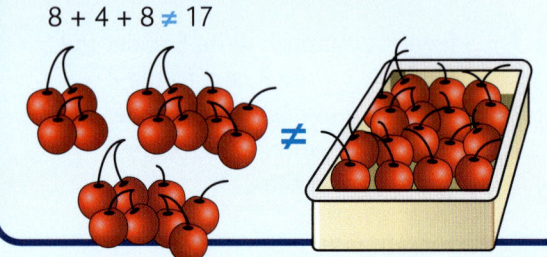

>

greater than   أكبر من

This sign means larger or *greater than*. So, in the example previous, you could use > :
8 + 4 + 8 = 20
20 > 17

<

less than   أقل من

This sign means smaller or *less than*. So, if Marie held only two cherries, while Ahmed held four, Walid held eight and Yasmin held seventeen:
2 + 4 + 8 = 14
14 < 17

≈

approximately equal to   يساوي تقريبًا

This sign represents approximately equal to. For example:
Rashid makes a 1 litre jug of fresh orange juice to share equally with three friends. However, the glasses that he has only hold just less than 25 cl each, so he is going to have a tiny bit left over.
If he wanted to present that in the form of a diagram, he could do so like this:

76

similar *adjective* مشابه / متشابه

Two plane figures with corresponding angles equal and corresponding sides proportional are defined as similar
Quadrilateral ABCD is *similar* to quadrilateral PORS.

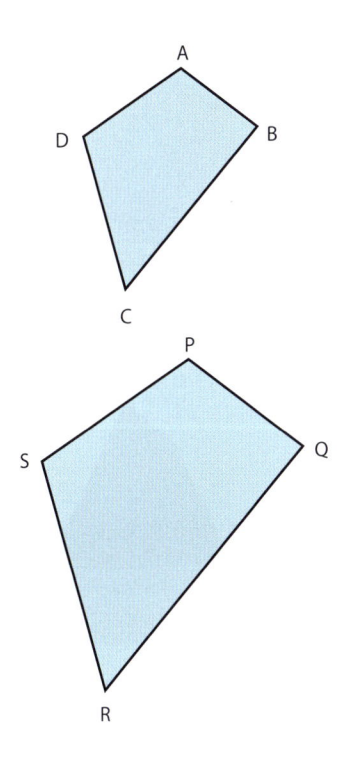

similar triangles
noun مثلثات متماثلة

Another term for equivalent triangles
See equivalent

slope

slant height
noun ارتفاع جانبي (مائل)

The slant height (*h*) of a cone is the distance from the vertex to the base measured along the surface

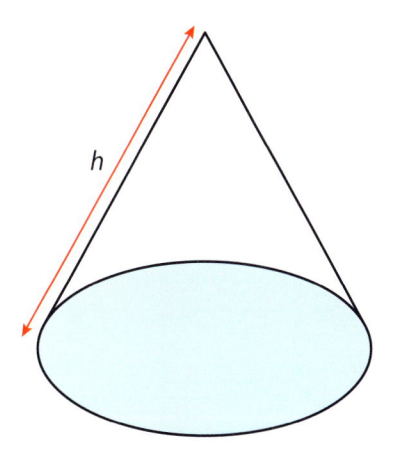

slope *noun* ميل

The slope of a straight line is the ratio of the 'rise' to the 'run' of any two points on the line

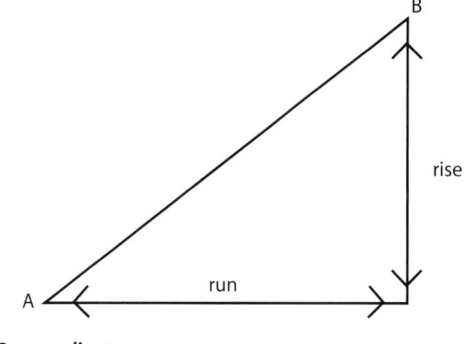

See gradient

solid or 3D shapes

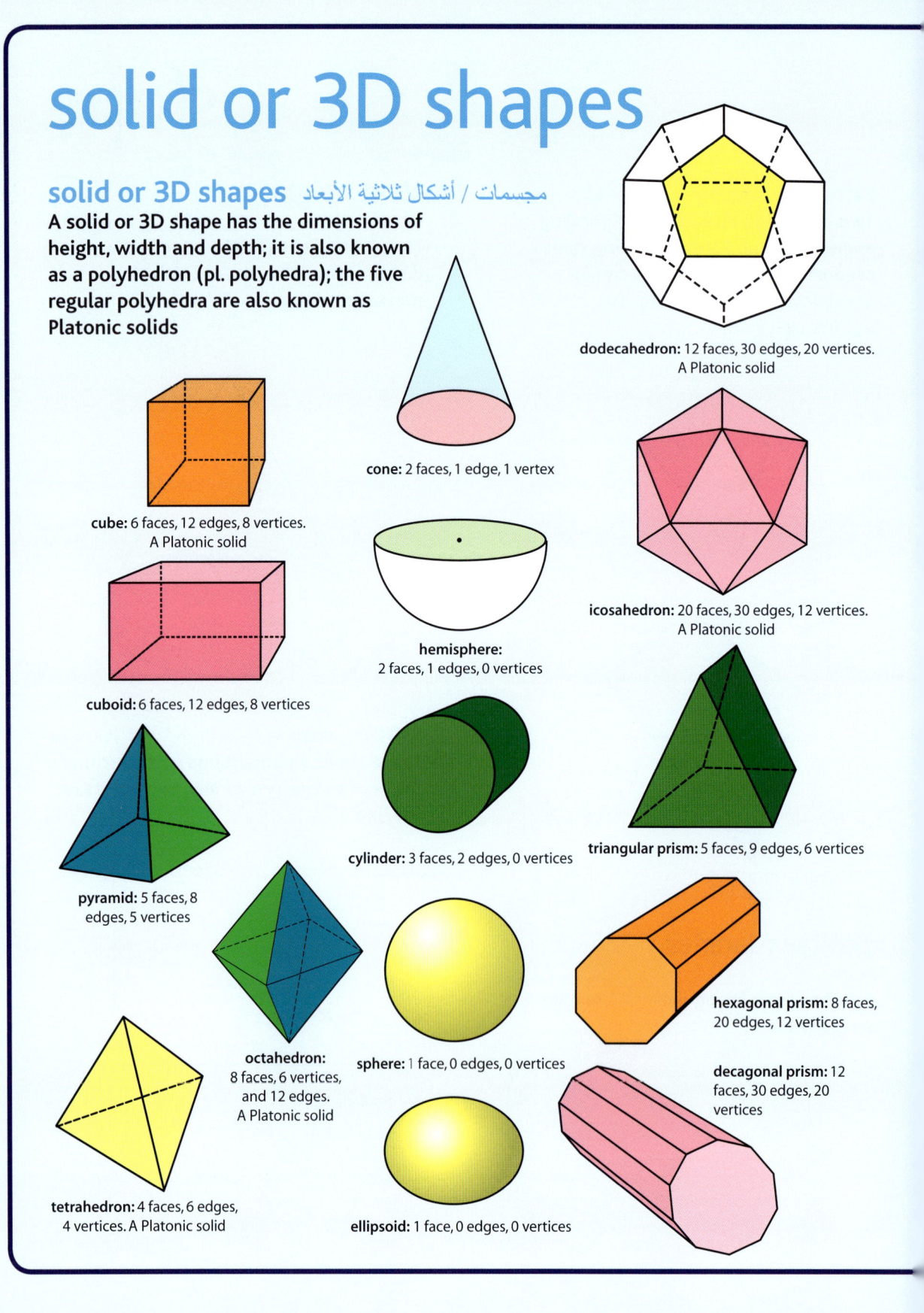

solid or 3D shapes مجسمات / أشكال ثلاثية الأبعاد
A solid or 3D shape has the dimensions of height, width and depth; it is also known as a polyhedron (pl. polyhedra); the five regular polyhedra are also known as Platonic solids

dodecahedron: 12 faces, 30 edges, 20 vertices. A Platonic solid

cone: 2 faces, 1 edge, 1 vertex

cube: 6 faces, 12 edges, 8 vertices. A Platonic solid

hemisphere: 2 faces, 1 edges, 0 vertices

icosahedron: 20 faces, 30 edges, 12 vertices. A Platonic solid

cuboid: 6 faces, 12 edges, 8 vertices

cylinder: 3 faces, 2 edges, 0 vertices

triangular prism: 5 faces, 9 edges, 6 vertices

pyramid: 5 faces, 8 edges, 5 vertices

hexagonal prism: 8 faces, 20 edges, 12 vertices

octahedron: 8 faces, 6 vertices, and 12 edges. A Platonic solid

sphere: 1 face, 0 edges, 0 vertices

decagonal prism: 12 faces, 30 edges, 20 vertices

tetrahedron: 4 faces, 6 edges, 4 vertices. A Platonic solid

ellipsoid: 1 face, 0 edges, 0 vertices

statistics

solution noun   الحل
In mathematics, the answer to a mathematical problem
For example, in the algebraic problem $5x + 3 = 18$, when you have found the value of x, you have found the *solution*.

space adjective   الفراغ
A three-dimensional (3D) region; the volume of an object can be defined as the amount of space it occupies
Space and volume are measured in cubic units such as cubic centimetres (cm^3) and cubic metres (m^3).
A box measuring 30 cm^3 would be too big to fit into a box measuring 20 cm^3, that is, it would take up too much *space*.
See volume

sphere noun   الكرة
A three-dimensional (3D) closed surface; every point on its surface is equidistant from its centre; a sphere has a radius r; the formula for the surface area of a sphere is $4\pi r^2$; the volume is $\frac{4}{3}\pi r^3$
Many balls, such as tennis balls and snooker balls, are examples of *spheres*.

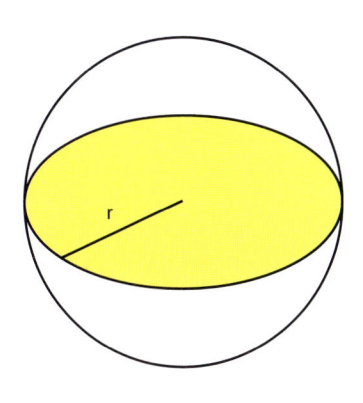

square noun/adjective   مربع
A two-dimensional (2D) figure with four equal sides and four right angles
For example, all four sides of a *square* table are the same length.
See plane or 2D shapes

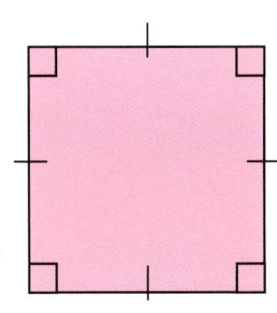

square number noun   عدد مربع
The product of two identical numbers
For example: $4 \times 4 = 16$ $4 \times 4 = 4^2 = 16$

square root noun   جذر تربيعي
The square root of a number is the number which can be multiplied by itself to produce the original number
The *square root* of 16 or $\sqrt{16}$ has two values; +4 and -4 because $(+4)^2 = 16$ and $(-4)^2 = 16$.

statistics noun   علم الإحصاء
The study and analysis of data and information in order to understand present-day situations and make forecasts about the future; this data is often shown on graphs
For example, if you were to gather *statistics* about your classmates' favourite sports, and then record this information on a pictograph, you would be able to see what the most popular sports were.
See graphs

79

straight

straight *adjective* مستقيم
A line of constant gradient is straight
The shortest distance between two points is always a *straight* line.
See gradient

subset *noun* مجموعة جزئية
A set within a wider set
A *subset* cannot contain any element which is not in the main set.
In the set of countries {France, Germany, Italy, Greece, United States, Syria, Turkey, Iran}, there is a *subset* of countries beginning with I {Italy, Iran}.
See set

substitution *noun* تعويض
Replacing a term in an equation or expression by another known value
For example:
If $x = 4$, then x can be *substituted* by 4 in
$2x + 3y = 20$:
$2x + 3y = 20$
$(2 \times 4) + 3y = 20$
$8 + 3y = 20$
$3y = 20 - 8$
$3y = 12$
$y = 4$
See equation

subtraction *noun* طرح
Calculating the difference between two numbers
$17 - 9 = 8$, is an example of *subtraction*.
See signs

subtrahend *noun* مطروح
A subtracted number.
In $17 - 9 = 8$, the *subtrahend* is 9, the difference is 8 and 17 is the minuend.
See difference, minuend, signs

sum *noun* ناتج الجمع
The result of addition also known as the total
For example:
In $9 + 8 = 17$, the *sum* or total is 17; the 9 and 8 are called addends.
See addend, addition, total

supplementary angles *noun* الزوايا المتكاملة
Angles whose sum is 180° or two right angles
Adjacent angles on a straight line are *supplementary*.
Compare complementary angles

surface *noun* سطح
A two-dimensional (2D) region; the amount of surface underlies the concept of are; surface and area are measured in square units such as square centimetres (cm^2) and square metres (m^2)
If a football pitch were 100 m long and 75 m wide, its *surface* would measure 7500 m^2.
See area

symbols

symbols *noun* رموز

A letter, letters or a sign used to represent a number or variable

( ) [ ] أقواس العمليات الحسابية

( ) (parentheses) and *[ ]* (square brackets) are used to group terms within an expression and indicate that whatever is in them must be dealt with first. For example:

7 - (7 - 3) $[(3 + 5) - 4]^3$
= 7 - 4 $= [8 - 4]^3$
= 3 $= 4^3$
               $= 64$

See order of operations

{ } أقواس المجموعة

Curly brackets *{ }* denote a set, for example:
J = {even numbers less than 14}
J = {2, 4, 6, 8, 10, 12}

U اتحاد

denotes union when dealing with sets.
For example:
if set X = {1, 3, 5, 7, 9} and Set Y = {3, 9, 15, 21} then X U Y = {1, 3, 5, 7, 9, 15, 21}.

ξ المجموعة الشاملة

denotes the universal set in Venn diagrams, that is, the set to which everything being discussed belongs

φ فاي / المجموعة الخالية

denotes a null set, or an empty set – a set that has no members
For example:
N = odd numbers ending in 2, N = φ

% النسبة المئوية

denotes per cent, for every hundred
For example:
24% = $\frac{24}{100}$ = 24 out of every hundred.

a^2 مربع / تربيع

represents a squared. Another way of saying this is a raised to the power of 2, that is, *a* x *a*

$a \times a = a^2$

a^3 represents a cubed. Another way of saying this is 'a raised to the power of 3', that is,
$a \times a \times a = a^3$
$a \times a \times a \times a = a^4$ and so on.
In each of these instances, the superscript number is known as the power, the exponent or the index.

√ الجذر التربيعي

denotes square root, for example
$\sqrt{16} = 4$, $\sqrt{9} = 3$, $\sqrt{a^2} = a$

π النسبة التقريبية للدائرة

denotes pi for the ratio of a circle's circumference to its diameter:
π is the symbol for the approximation of 3.142 or $\frac{22}{7}$ as a value for the variables $\frac{c}{d}$, standing for the circumference and diameter of a circle in

$\frac{\text{circumference}}{\text{diameter}}$ = π or C = π diameter

81

symmetry

symmetry *noun*   تماثل

A flat or 2D shape exhibits symmetry when it can be folded so that one part exactly covers the other; a line of symmetry can be identified where one side of the shape is a mirror image of the other

Many things in nature are *symmetrical*, for instance butterflies.

See asymmetry, line of symmetry, reflection

symmetry

Many regular shapes are *symmetrical*.

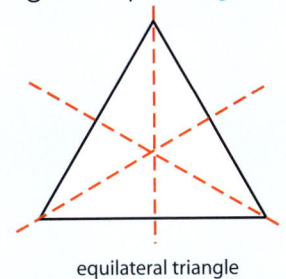

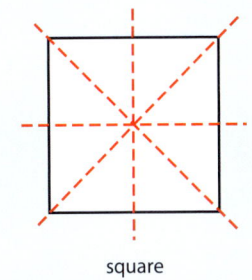

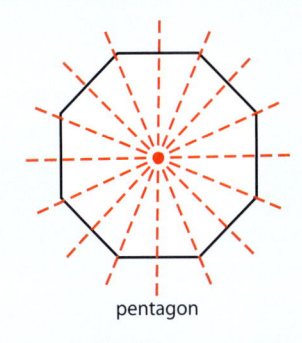

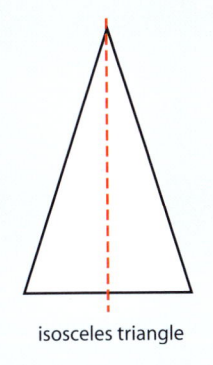

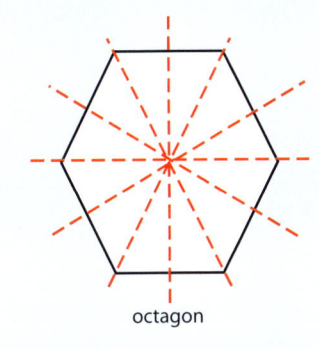

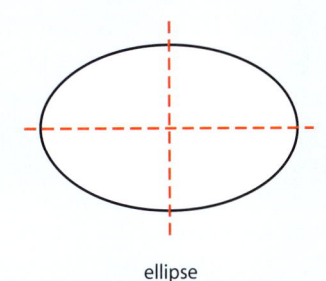

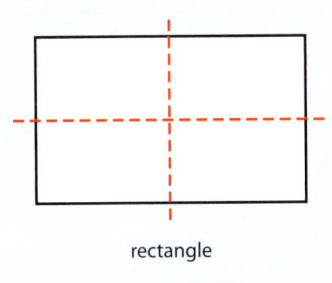

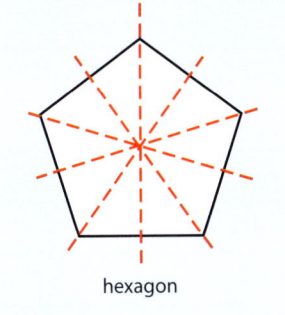

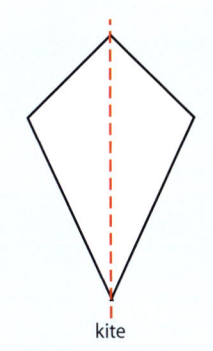

equilateral triangle   square   pentagon

isosceles triangle   octagon   ellipse

rectangle   hexagon   kite

Some letters are *symmetrical*, but not all.

A B C D E F G H I J
K L M N O P Q R S
T U V W X Y Z

83

system

system *noun* نظام

A system such as the base ten system. Numbers in the base 10 system are grouped in ones, tens, hundreds ... or 1, 10, 100, 1000 ... or $10^0, 10^1, 10^2, 10^3$ ... Similarly numbers in base 2 or the binary *system* are grouped in ones, twos, fours, eights ... or 1, 2, 4, 8 ... or $2^0, 2^1, 2^2, 2^3$ ...

See base, decimal, hexadecimal

Système International (SI)

noun النظام الدولي للوحدات / النظام المتري

From the French: Système International d'unites, also known as the 'International System of Units' or SI – is the modern form of the metric system

See metric and SI units

Important SI base units

	Symbol	What it Measures
ampere	A	electric current
kilogram	kg	mass
Kelvin	K	temperature
metre	m	length
second	s	time

Tt

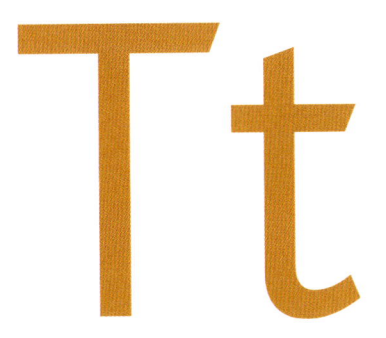

table *noun* جدول
A list of numbers or other information arranged in rows and columns

This is the multiplication table up to 6 x 6

x	1	2	3	4	5	6
1	1	2	3	4	5	6
2	2	4	6	8	10	12
3	3	6	9	12	15	18
4	4	8	12	16	20	24
5	5	10	15	20	25	30
6	6	12	18	24	30	36

take away *verb* يطرح
To remove items or numbers by subtracting them; the - sign shows that one number is being taken away from another
24 *take away* 16 equals 8
24 - 16 = 8
This could also be said 24 subtract 16 equals 8, or 24 minus 16 equals 8.
See signs, subtraction

tally *noun/verb* علامة تدل على التكرار
A score or account made using marks rather than numbers initially
So where something has been tallied, each time it is counted, a single mark is made. Marks are made in groups of 4, and then the 5th mark is made as a line through the first 4 marks, for example:

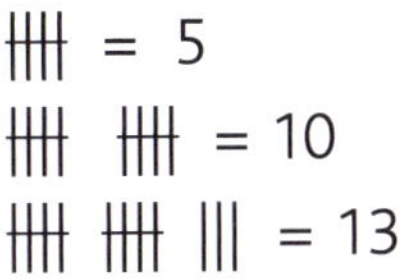

⦀⦀ = 5
⦀⦀ ⦀⦀ = 10
⦀⦀ ⦀⦀ ||| = 13

tangent *noun* مماس
In a right-angled triangle, the tangent of an acute angle is the ratio of the side opposite the given angle to the adjacent side; a tangent is a line that just touches a curve but does not cross it

$$\tan x = \frac{\text{opposite}}{\text{adjacent}}$$

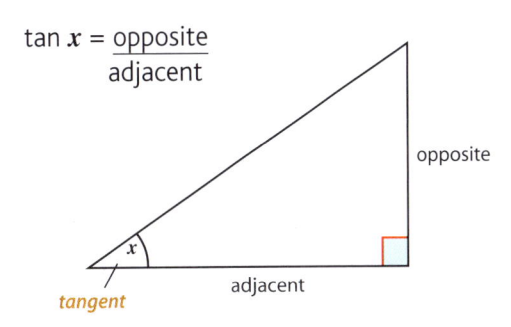

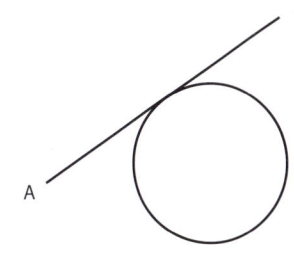

AB is a *tangent* to the circle.

tera-

tera-
prefix   تيرا : بادئة بمعنى مليون مليون

Used in front of units to multiply that unit by 10 to the power of 12, making it a very large number

10^{12} = 1 000 000 000 000

1 *terabyte* is equal to 1024 gigabytes

term   *noun*   حَد / طرَف

Part of an expression, equation or sequence

3   8   13   18   23   ...   ...

The next two *terms* in this sequence are 28 and 33.

See sequence

tessellation   *noun*   ترصيع

A pattern made by fitting plane shapes together without gaps

When the pattern uses just one regular plane shape it is called a regular *tessellation* (like wall tiles in a bathroom). If more than one shape is used (such as on a football) it is called an irregular *tessellation*.

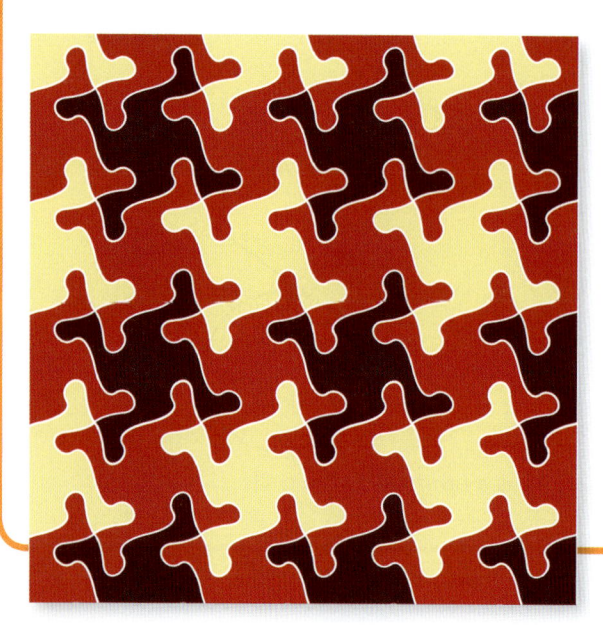

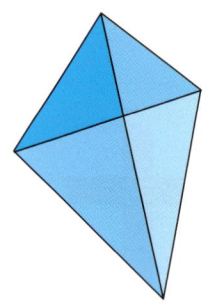

tetrahedron
noun   رباعي الوجوه (هرم ثلاثي)

A solid shape with four triangular faces

A regular *tetrahedron* is one of only five regular polyhedra (also known as Platonic solids) as each of the four faces is an equilateral triangle.

See solid or 3D shapes

time   *noun*   الزمن

A period or occasion measured in seconds, minutes, hours, days and years

The *time* shown on this clock is 2:40.

See calendar

tonne   *noun*   طن

A unit of metric measurement of mass or weight

1 tonne is 1000 kilograms

1 tonne = 1000 kg

torus *noun* الطارة
A solid ring shape with a hole in the middle
A *doughnut* is a torus shape.

total *noun* كل/ مجموع
The result when you add together a group of numbers
The *total* of the first 4 odd numbers is 16
1 + 3 + 5 + 7 = 16

Tower of Hanoi
noun برج هانوي
A mathematical puzzle invented in 1883, sometimes called the Tower of Brahma; the simplest version consists of three pegs with discs of different sizes which can fit onto the pegs
The objective of the puzzle is to move the discs from one peg to the other side, obeying these rules:
- move one top disc at a time
- no disc can go on top of a smaller disc

transversal

transformation
noun تحويلة هندسية
A change made to the position and/or size of a shape
Enlargement, reflection, rotation and translation are all examples of *transformations*.
See reflection, rotation, translation

translation *noun* انتقال / إزاحة
A transformation in a straight line, so that every point of a shape moves the same distance and direction

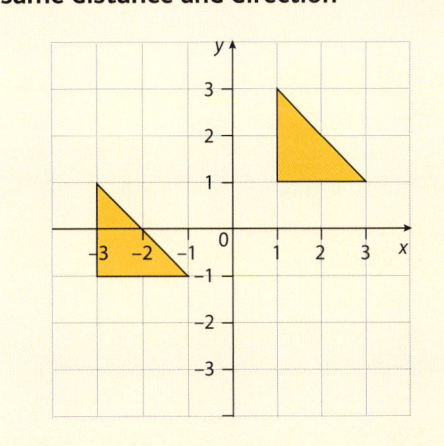

transversal *adjective* قاطع
A line which cuts across two or more other lines

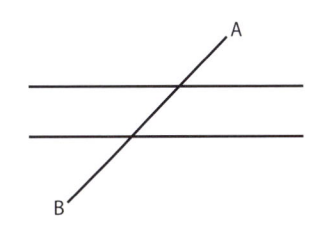

AB is a *transversal* line.

87

trapezium

trapezium *noun*   شبه منحرف
A quadrilateral with one pair of parallel sides
A *trapezium* can have two right angles.

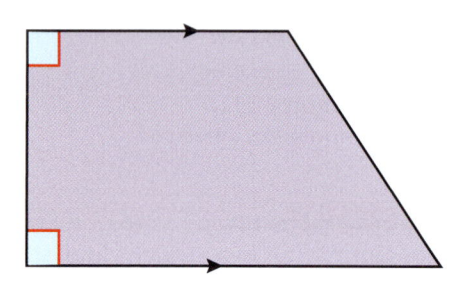

See plane or 2D shapes

triangle *noun*   مثلث
A 3-sided polygon
The three angles of a *triangle* always add up to 180°.

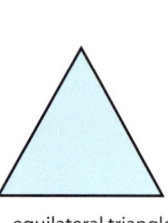

equilateral triangle   isosceles triangle

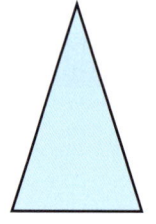

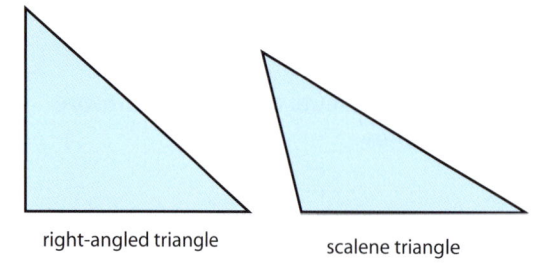

right-angled triangle   scalene triangle

See plane or 2D shapes

triangular number *noun*   عدد مثلث
A number that can be arranged as a triangle with a group of dots
The sequence begins 1, 3, 6, 10, 15, 21, 28 …

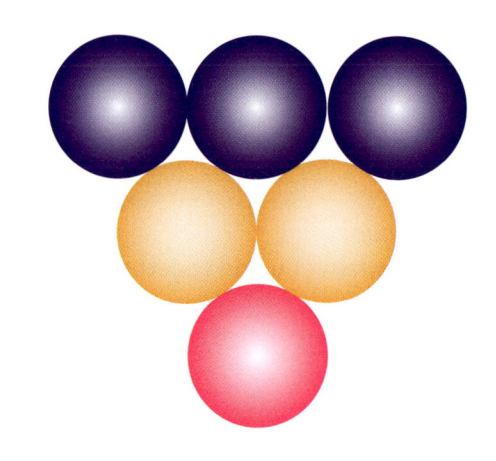

6 is a *triangular number*

Uu

union *noun* اتحاد

As in A U B – 'set A union set B'
If A = {1, 2, 3, 4, 5} and B = {3, 4, 7, 11, 18} the *union* of A and B can be shown by this Venn diagram.

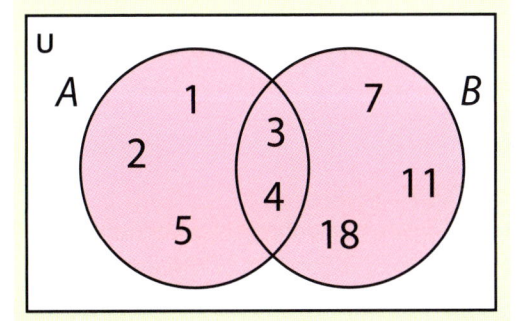

A U B = {1, 2, 3, 4, 5, 7, 11, 18}
Elements or members 3 and 4 appear only once in A U B. ξ denotes the universal set in Venn diagrams.
See universal set, Venn diagram

unit *noun* وحدة

Another name for any number below 10
In the base 10 system the *units* are between the tens and the tenths.
For example, the number 23 represents 2 tens and 3 *units* or ones.

10^9	10^8	10^7	10^6	10^5	10^4	10^3	10^2	10^1	10^0	10^{-1}	10^{-2}	10^{-3}
Billion	Hundred-millions	Ten-millions	Millions	Hundred-thousands	Ten-thousands	Thousands	Hundreds	Tens	Units	Tenths	Hundredths	Thousandths

units *noun* وحدات

The basic metric units of length, mass and time are the metre (m), kilogram (kg) and second (s); units of area, volume, density and speed are based on these
See metric and SI units, Système international (SI)

universal set *noun* المجموعة الشاملة

A set to which all the objects to be discussed belong and denoted in Venn diagrams by ξ
See set, subset, Venn diagram

89

Vv

value   noun   قيمة
Each digit in any number in any base has a place value; the value for each part of the number is a multiple of the base number

2^6	2^5	2^4	2^3	2^2	2^1	2^0	2^{-1}	2^{-2}	2^{-3}
Sixty-fours	Thirty-twos	Sixteens	Eights	Fours	Twos	Units	Halves	Quarters	Eighths

This diagram shows the place *values* for base 2.

variable   noun   متغير
A symbol or symbols which represent numbers or values
The formula:
Area = length x breadth can be written as
$A = l \times b$, where *l* and *b* are *variables*.

The formula:
Volume = length x breadth x height can be written as $V = l \times b \times h$, where *l*, *b* and *h* are *variables*.
See formula

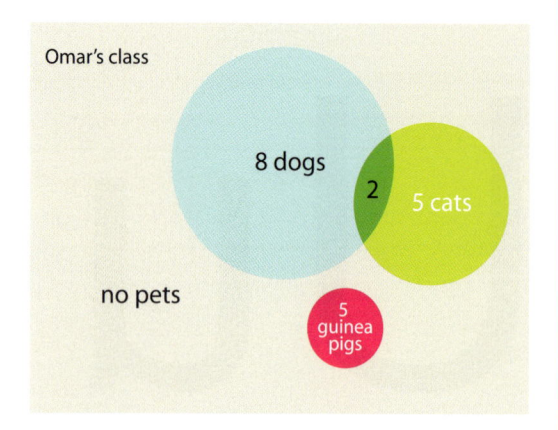

Venn diagram   noun   أشكال فن
A diagram made up of rectangles and circles which shows the elements of sets and their relationships
In Omar's class 20 of the students have pets and 10 do not. Of the 20 who did, 10 have dogs, 7 have cats, 5 have guinea pigs only and 2 students have a dog and a cat. This information can be shown in the *Venn diagram* above.
See set, union

vertex   noun   رأس
In 2D figures or polygons, a vertex (pl. vertices) is formed at the intersection of adjacent sides
In 3D figures or polyhedra, a *vertex* is formed at the intersection of planes.

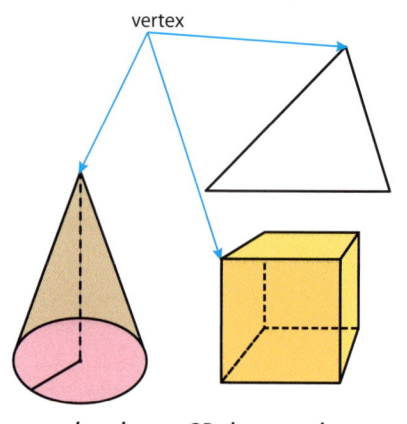

See cone, cube, plane or 2D shapes, polygon, polyhedron, solid or 3D shapes

whole number

vertical *adjective*   عمودي / رأسي
Perpendicular to the plane of the horizon
A graph's '*y*-axis' is the *vertical* axis. It is at right angles or perpendicular to the horizontal '*x*-axis'.
See axis

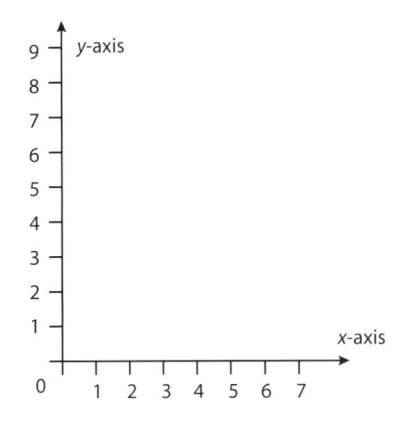

volume *noun*   حجم
While area is the amount of 2D surface, volume is the amount of 3D space
The *volume* of an object can be defined as the amount of space it occupies.
Space and *volume* are measured in cubic units such as cubic centimetres (cm^3) and cubic metres (m^3), and can be calculated using formulae.
See formula, space

vulgar fraction *noun*   كسر غير حقيقي
In vulgar or improper fractions the denominator is less than the numerator
For example:
$\frac{3}{2}$ and $\frac{6}{4}$ are *vulgar* or improper fractions.
See fraction, improper fraction

Ww

weight *noun*   وزن
The gravitational force acting on a body
The *weight* of a body on the surface of the Moon is $\frac{1}{6}$ th of its *weight* on the Earth due to the Moon's gravitation being $\frac{1}{6}$ th of the Earth's. Formally, *weight* should be expressed as a force in Newtons (N).
In everyday use on Earth, *weight* is commonly used to mean the heaviness of the object, measured in - tonnes (t), kilograms (kg) and grams (g).
See mass

whole number *noun*
عدد من مجموعة الأعداد الطبيعية والصفر
All counting numbers or natural numbers or positive integers together with zero
The set of counting numbers = {1, 2, 3, 4, 5...}
The set of whole numbers = {0, 1, 2, 3, 4, 5...}
See integer

91

Xx

x symbol
الرمز المقابل لـ "س"

A symbol which is commonly used in algebra to denote an unknown number

For example in $3x = 21$, x is an unknown value. In this case, $x = 7$.

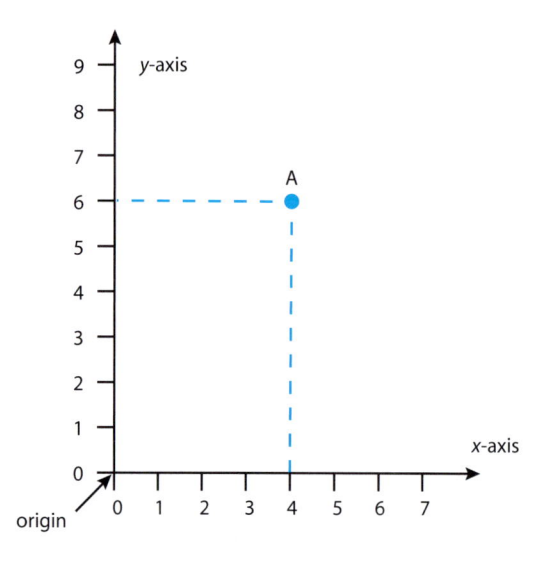

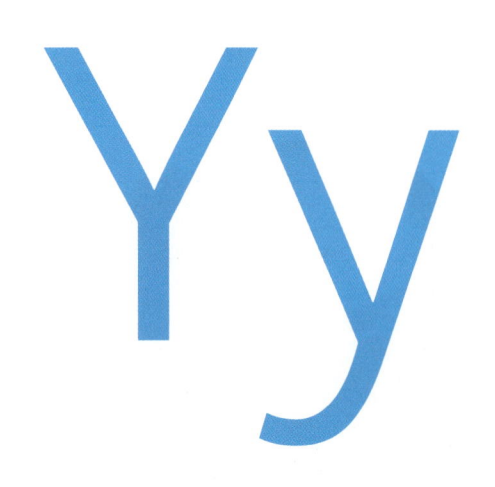

x and y axes
noun   المحوران السيني والصادي

The x-axis is the horizontal axis and shows the range of values of the independent variable; the y-axis is the vertical axis and shows the range of values of the dependent variable

By referring to the scales on the *x-and y-axes*, the position of A can be written as (4, 6).

The '*x-axis*' reference, also known as the x-coordinate or abscissa is always written first. The '*y-axis*' reference, also known as the y-coordinate or ordinate is the second entry.

See axis

Yy

y symbol
الرمز المقابل لـ "ص"

A symbol which is commonly used in algebra to denote an unknown number

For example in $2y + 1 = 25$, y is an unknown value. In this case $y = 12$.

Zz

Zeno *noun*   زينو: فيلسوف يوناني

A famous philosopher who lived in Greece in the 5th century BC

One of *Zeno's* famous 'paradoxes' involves Achilles and a tortoise, who are going to run a race. Achilles feels confident about winning and gives the tortoise a start.

Zeno describes how Achilles can never pass the tortoise by saying that before he overtakes the tortoise, he must first run to point A, where the tortoise started. But then the tortoise has crawled to point B. Now Achilles must run to point B. But the tortoise has gone to point C, etc. Achilles is stuck in a situation in which he gets closer and closer to the tortoise, but never catches him and so cannot win the race.

Zeno has divided Achilles' race into an infinite number of parts. He must pass point A, then B, then C, etc. *Zeno* argues that you can't do an infinite number of tasks in a finite amount of time.

See finite, infinte

zero *noun*   الصفر

Part of the set of whole numbers for which the value is nothing

The Hindus in India had symbols for the numerals 1 to 9 over 2000 years ago.

The Arabs developed the Hindus' numerals and added a symbol for 0.

The inclusion of *zero* enables numbers to be written which have *zero* as a place value holder.

For example: 100 means 1 hundred, 0 tens and 0 units. The *zeros* have an important place value function.

See Hindu Arabic, place value, whole numbers

Zeno.
(Visconti, Icon. greca.)